Self-Advocacy

Your Guide to Getting What You Deserve at Work

Shailvi Wakhlu

Praise for Self-Advocacy by Shailvi Wakhlu

"A great read! Shailvi does a masterful job of bringing simplicity to a complex topic and outlining self-advocacy steps anyone can apply to their careers and life."
—**Mark Gainey**, Chairman & Co-Founder at Strava

"Shailvi's work on self-advocacy is more than mere guidance; it's a distillation of hard-earned wisdom and courage from years within the industry. Her masterclass on growing your career through self-advocacy is inspiring; it's essential reading for anyone seeking to grow their career with authenticity and strength."
—**Mike Micucci**, CEO Fabric Commerce

"We aren't born with innate skills of self-advocacy. The author shares how to develop your personal skillset. Whether you're hoping for the corner office, the boardroom, or personal fulfillment, this book will fast track your success. Stop allowing opportunities to slip away. Apply the insights within these pages and transform your work, and your life!"
—**Lois Creamer**, Book More Business

"Self-Advocacy by Shailvi Wakhlu not only empowers individuals but also equips leaders to cultivate diverse teams. This book provides actionable strategies for navigating career landscapes while embracing the power of advocacy and collaboration. A must-read for those championing workplace inclusivity."
—**Amy C. Waninger**, CEO, Lead at Any Level

"Self-advocacy may not come easy for many, but it's the best way to let others know your value. Shailvi's book will help you grow from complaining to those who can't help you to influencing those who can. Definitely worth a read!"
—**Neil Thompson**, Founder of Teach the Geek

"Developing self-advocacy skills is an important investment for our careers. And for women working in male-dominated fields, it's essential. Wakhlu's book provides a framework for everyday self-advocacy, as well as for landing important milestones such as promotions, raises, and job offers."
—**Karen Catlin**, author of *Better Allies*

Self-Advocacy

Your Guide to Getting What You Deserve at Work

by

Shailvi Wakhlu

Printed in the United States of America

First Printing, 2023

ISBN: 978-1-953640-23-9 (hardcover)
ISBN: 978-1-953640-22-2 (paperback)
ISBN: 978-1-953640-24-6 (Kindle edition)
Library of Congress Control Number: 2023915615

A Page Beyond
11650 Olio Road, Suite 1000 #392
Fishers, IN 46037
www.APageBeyond.com

a page beyond

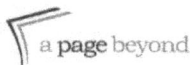

Ordering Information:
Special discounts are available on quantity purchases by corporations, associations, and others who purchase directly from the author. Contact shailvi@shailvi.com for details.

For Govind.

Your endless support, encouragement,

and love since the day we first met are

what make my life beautiful.

Contents

Introduction
My Story

In the summer of 2019, I experienced my professional career's most significant inflection point. I had a job I loved at a highly regarded Fortune 500 company. My work was stellar, and my stakeholders were thrilled. But I wasn't happy. The executive in charge of our division did not have the right leadership team in place. The chaos that resulted was limiting my growth. So, I undertook a radical act of self-advocacy. Armed with a 72-page pitch deck, I requested an audit and overhaul of our department's leadership. Here I was, taking on a powerful executive, hoping to create meaningful change within an organization I valued.

My effort wasn't just about my promotion, growth opportunities, or poor working conditions. Instead, my mission was to change how the entire department was being run, to create the psychological safety required for all of us to do our best work. In addition to my pitch deck, I had the attention of Human Resources (HR) leaders, the quiet encouragement of my colleagues, and the moral support of many stakeholders who loved my work. Advocating for oneself can have impacts far beyond an individual, addressing the needs of an entire collective.

Was my self-advocacy successful? It depends on how you look at it! On the one hand, HR acknowledged and agreed with many of my concerns. They said they had every intention to dig deeper. I was inspired by and grateful for my willingness and ability to fight for myself and others. On the other hand, the investigation took nearly a year to reach a reasonable conclusion. While my efforts produced better outcomes for many, the lengthy process evoked emotional, mental, and sometimes physical distress for me. I had the will to stick it out and the knowledge that self-advocacy was a worthy goal. But I didn't have the tools I needed to protect myself along the way. My victory came at a significant personal cost.

After six months of fighting the good fight, I was emotionally drained. I worried my career would suffer if I were stuck in professional limbo for too long. Although I might have gotten the outcome I desired had I waited another six months, I decided to leave the company and protect my peace. After a short break, I landed one of my best career roles at a small health-tech startup.

Between those jobs, I presented a talk, *How to #HumbleBrag Effectively,* at the Write Speak Code conference. I drew on my experiences working and advocating for myself in tech. Nearly one hundred people attended the session, and the response was overwhelmingly positive! Clearly, my content had struck a chord with others who had felt sidelined in our industry.

Over the next four years, I continued to speak on self-advocacy, all while working full-time in the tech sector. I initially thought this message would only resonate with people from underrepresented genders in tech. Wrong! I've since learned that people everywhere struggle with speaking up for themselves.

During a talk I delivered in Budapest, I shared that some leaders may not struggle with self-advocacy, especially if they don't belong to an underrepresented group. Afterward, an audience member asked me to reconsider that assumption. He told me that, even as a white man in tech working in Europe, he didn't have the right tools to advocate for himself in an authentic way. Because self-advocacy skills aren't part of the training for early career professionals, many people lack these skills.

I have been giving talks to people all over the world, and it has helped me make this book better. I am a Data & Analytics leader and have used and improved these ideas for my job. I have also been a mentor to over three hundred people, helping them with their careers. Listening to their stories and problems has shaped how I see things too. Some said they felt ignored in meetings, while others were upset seeing others get promotions while they worked harder. People often told me they had trouble finding the right words or feeling brave enough to share their thoughts. I want to thank everyone for being honest and specific in our conversations. Your stories led me to write this book, and I am so grateful for you. You reminded me that this topic is essential, and I am happy to have invested my energy to further these learnings through this book.

It has also been heartwarming to hear updates from the people I've met along the way. For many, the simple shift of adopting a self-advocacy mindset was a huge victory. People shared that they now track their wins weekly (or even daily). Some told me how sharing suggestions with their teams improved their work environment. My favorite stories are always from people who didn't think speaking up would make a difference but tried anyway and got what they needed! I am inspired by those who have used our conversations as the launch pad for pay raises and promotions. Hearing these stories has reminded me to keep prioritizing my own goals!

I focused on self-advocacy before, during, and after that summer in 2019. My next role was at a health-tech startup. There, I used these skills to deliver one of the best pitches of my career for a promotion, as my boss at the time described it. Later, I advocated for a 60 percent salary increase for one of my team members. When it was time to move into a fitness-tech role, I successfully negotiated a higher title and position than the company initially offered.

I also ruthlessly prioritized the success of my team. Several new employees had listed salary expectations below their market value. I ensured the company paid them fairly with my advocacy, although it was more than they had asked for. Advocating for my team also made my job easier. Even during the Great Resignation, my team's turnover rate was under 2 percent! At my core, I hope to remain a technologist who will always advocate for herself. Of equal importance, I am proud to be a leader with a reputation for caring deeply and acting in the best interests of her team.

Over my career of more than sixteen years, I have advocated successfully for my promotions (sometimes a few short months after starting a new job), raises, job offers, professional growth opportunities, and more. I've also prioritized breaks for my mental wellness and pushed for workplace accommodations for myself and others. There is no magic formula that works every time. With practice, I've learned to maximize my chances of success—without letting the process emotionally drain me, regardless of the outcome.

While it may seem that advocating for myself comes naturally, that wasn't true for most of my life. In this book, I'll expose everything I have had to unlearn about my default mindset that hindered self-advocacy. I'll share how I learned to prioritize and effectively articulate my needs. I'll provide all the tools I've used to better position myself in the workplace. And finally, I'll help you commit to building your self-advocacy muscle consistently and intentionally.

Whether this book is for you or for someone you know, I hope that it:

- ✓ Leads you to your authentic voice, one that speaks up when you need it.
- ✓ Normalizes prioritizing what you want and going after it with intention.
- ✓ Helps you ask for what you need without guilt.
- ✓ Helps you to get measurably better at advocating for yourself!

Chapter 1
What Is Self-Advocacy?

Each day, we come across situations that impact our well-being in various ways. These situations may influence how easily we can perform our tasks at work, the happiness we find in our work environment, the sense of achievement when our efforts are recognized and praised, the contentment of using our skills effectively, or simply the comfort of being treated fairly.

When we go through these experiences, we often seek support from others who can help us. It might be our manager that speaks up for us, or aids our growth by connecting us to opportunities we are interested in pursuing. It could be the coworker that champions our team's needs. Sometimes it is our department leader who notices and praises our efforts. These individuals are our advocates. Whether they do it consciously or not, they take actions that benefit us. Such advocacy makes our work lives smoother and more fulfilling. Almost everyone desires such advocates at work and actively looks for them!

Sadly, not everyone has advocates or sponsors at their workplace. There are a few reasons for this. For example, you might be part of a very large team, making it difficult for your manager to address each person's needs individually, leading them to focus more on the group as a whole. Another possibility is that the right people who could advocate for you may not fully understand the significance of your work. It's also possible that you have people who could advocate for you but choose not to for various reasons. They might recognize your value and the importance of your work, yet they either need to be prompted to advocate for you or only do so when they can see a clear benefit for themselves.

This book focuses on self-advocacy, which means learning how to speak up for yourself and positively impact the outcomes that affect you and your life. There are moments when you can influence situations to your benefit. It's essential to consider how often you feel confident enough to express your preferences. Do you feel comfortable making a case for why your needs should be considered? And do you naturally highlight your contributions to present them in the best possible way? This book aims to help you improve your ability to advocate for yourself and achieve better results.

Self-advocacy is speaking up for oneself and one's best interest.

Self-advocacy means acting when we have a chance to influence something that is advantageous for us. It's about making sure we don't pass up the opportunity to speak up and bring about positive change, especially when staying silent might not lead to the best outcome for us. In such situations, self-advocacy involves intentionally raising our voices to make a difference and bring about the desired changes.

How often do you advocate for yourself in the situations listed in the following worksheet? Some of these examples may not apply to you. Regardless, they will help you consider what self-advocacy at work could look like for you. You can download this worksheet, along with other tools, at www.shailvi.com/self-advocacy-resources.html.

	Always	Sometimes	Never	Not applicable
1. Correcting people when they mispronounce your name				
2. Reminding people to use your correct pronouns or title				
3. Reminding people that certain times are off-limits for you due to your caregiving responsibilities				
4. Taking time off when you need to recharge and disconnect				
5. Declining extra work when your bandwidth is at its limit				
6. Letting people know you found a joke they shared to be offensive				
7. Not giving in to peer pressure when it conflicts with your preferences or values				
8. Asking for a workplace accommodation due to your disability or other need				
9. Declining when someone asks you for a favor that you are unable or unwilling to do				
10. Asking for better opportunities at work				

	Always	Sometimes	Never	Not applicable
11. Asking for useful feedback that helps you improve your work performance				
12. Asking to be mentored				
13. Asking to be paired with teammates you can learn from				
14. Asking to lead a project				
15. Asking for visibility and attribution for your work				
16. Asking for a promotion				
17. Asking for a raise				
18. Asking to switch teams when your current team limits your skill growth				
19. Asking to switch managers if your current manager is not a great fit				
20. Applying for other jobs when the current one doesn't meet your needs				

Take a moment to reflect on the results you've already gotten with your self-advocacy in these or other situations. What's going well? What are you proud of?

_____

_____

_____

_____

Where would you like to improve in your self-advocacy?

_____

_____

_____

_____

Types of Self-Advocacy

There are generally two main types of self-advocacy, proactive and reactive. Both approaches require you to have the right mindset, proper tools, and adequate practice to be successful.

Proactive Self-Advocacy

Proactive self-advocacy means acting in situations where you know that how you present yourself is important. By advocating for yourself ahead of time, you aim to increase your chances of achieving success.

These situations often arise in the workplace and may happen regularly or on a predictable schedule:

- A daily team update session (called a 'stand-up' in some companies) where you are expected to give brief updates about your work
- A weekly one-on-one meeting with your manager, where you talk about your work progress, the challenges you are facing, and/or career topics
- Quarterly or annual performance reviews with a self-assessment component
- A casual lunch-room chat with a coworker who asks what you are working on

In these situations and others, you have a choice either to downplay your accomplishments or to highlight the excellent work you do. When you opt for the latter, you are increasing the likelihood that your actions will positively impact your career in a significant manner.

Reactive Self-Advocacy

Reactive self-advocacy involves situations where you come across something that isn't in your best interest. When this happens, you have the option to speak up for yourself and try to make the situation better to meet your needs.

These situations might be unexpected, catching you off guard. Alternatively, they could be situations that have been gradually worsening over time, reaching a point where you feel the urge to take action and make a change.

- A shifting expectation where you are increasingly expected to work longer hours with no additional perks
- A reduction in your learning budget or the loss of some other perk that is meaningful to you
- A realization that you are paid a lower salary than your co-workers with similar skills and experiences
- A change in your family or caregiver status that makes flexible or remote work a priority

These situations occur when you have a specific need that isn't being fulfilled. In such cases, you have three choices: you can try to change the situation, look for a different situation that meets your needs better, or accept the situation, either with contentment or resentment. I call these options "the fight, flight, or freeze response." Different choices may be suitable for different situations and times. However, it's beneficial to learn the skills to assert yourself in situations where fighting for your needs is the only option. The term "fight" doesn't necessarily mean confrontational or filled with conflict. Instead, it's more like a dance, where you prepare and execute your actions to the best of your ability, increasing the chances of achieving a positive outcome.

Self-Advocacy in the Workplace

Self-advocacy plays a vital role in building your career and finding contentment in your work. A successful career involves demonstrating your value to the right people at the right time, and this requires being purposeful in your actions. Sometimes, you may be fortunate to have people who actively support and promote your work, but that's not always guaranteed and is still relatively uncommon. Taking control of your career is the best way to increase your chances of achieving the outcomes you desire. Learning how to showcase the work you're already doing and presenting it in the best possible way to the right people is a valuable skill to develop.

Self-advocacy also means being at ease with how you present yourself in a way that feels genuine. If it feels challenging or unfamiliar, it can be tough. But if you take the time to comprehend why it's difficult for you, you can assess those reasons and see if they hold true. Understanding how self-advocacy will benefit you personally can motivate you to create a deliberate plan for it. Once you learn how to effectively be your own best advocate, you can make significant progress in taking control of your career path.

Putting your needs first at work doesn't only impact your professional life but also has ripple effects on your personal life. If you feel unhappy or dissatisfied with your job, those negative feelings might carry over into your home life. Being overworked and burnt out can take a toll on your health and well-being. Feeling undervalued or inadequately compensated can lead to resentment towards your employer. Additionally, if you don't have opportunities to grow and develop your skills at work, it can make it more challenging to find better job prospects in the future.

In the end, self-advocacy is an action you take for yourself. It's about ensuring your happiness, advancing your career, and caring for your loved ones whose well-being is important to you. It aligns with your values and passions. Prioritizing your needs is like exercising a muscle that allows you to invest in your future, find happiness, and maintain your well-being!

Self-Advocacy as a Collective Pursuit

In self-advocacy, the "self" refers to you as an individual, but individuals are often part of a larger group. You may have a family, loved ones, or a team where their success impacts your own success. Similarly, in a community, everyone benefits when everyone succeeds. When you advocate for those who bring you joy, you're also advocating for things that bring you joy. Helping someone you care about succeed and advocate for themselves is also a form of self-advocacy because their success brings happiness and benefits to you too.

Advocating for yourself doesn't always mean you're the only one who gains from it. Others can benefit too. When you speak up, you might pave the way for someone else to follow a similar path. Also, you could be enlightening those in positions of power about needs they hadn't considered, leading to solutions that benefit everyone. Shedding light on important matters, even if they primarily affect you, benefits everyone in society. It builds community, drives innovation, and helps us progress together.

Whenever you advocate for yourself, it's not a negative thing for others. Neither the person you're asking nor any bystander loses anything when you stand up for yourself. Prioritizing your needs doesn't mean you're disregarding the needs of others. Requesting what you deserve or need doesn't automatically inconvenience someone else. Fairness isn't a limited resource, and asking to be treated fairly doesn't take away from what others deserve.

Set a Baseline

Before we delve into the other insights in this book, let's begin by establishing a starting point for what self-advocacy means to each of us. What does self-advocacy look like for you? Can you think of examples of situations where you can and should advocate for your best interests? Are there instances where you are already advocating for yourself and want to continue doing so?

These situations can be part of your daily life or specific milestones where you want to achieve the best outcome possible. Some might require you to be proactive and well-prepared, while others are situations where you'd like to do the right thing for yourself if the chance arises. Some things may only benefit you, while others could also benefit those you care about.

Make a list of these situations and imagine a world where you take charge of things that could benefit you. If you need ideas, you can refer to the list we began in Chapter 1 (*see page 13*) and jot down the ones that apply to you. Aim to write down at least ten items to get started. You can download a copy of this worksheet at www.shailvi.com/self-advocacy-resources.html.

1. _____

2. _____

3. _____

4. _____

5. _____

6. _____

7. _____

8. _____

9. _____

10. _____

Place a checkmark next to any of the above scenarios in which you are already advocating for yourself.

How many of these did you check?

2 or fewer: You are at the start of your journey. Congratulations on identifying that you want to invest further!

3 to 5: You have made some progress on self-advocacy. You have a foundation to build on, and you're ready to go further.

6 to 7: You are well on your way to mastering the key skills of self-advocacy! Use the momentum you've created to apply these skills where you need them most.

8 or more: You have mastered many self-advocacy skills that you consider crucial. You will soon reach a point where you are so confident in your self-advocacy that it becomes second nature for you!

As you continue to make progress and engage with the insights from this book, revisit the list you created. Take note of the items that are still on your list and that you need to improve upon. Also, think about new areas of self-advocacy that you want to become better at. It's essential to keep track of your growth and identify areas where you can further develop your skills.

Chapter 2
Why Is Self-Advocacy Difficult?

Quite a few of us grew up in an environment where advocating for ourselves wasn't seen as normal. It might have gone against what we were taught and the usual ways of interacting with others. If you were raised around people who didn't view speaking up for yourself positively, you might adopt similar beliefs. It's natural to feel uncertain about self-advocacy if its significance was never emphasized.

If you find self-advocacy to be difficult, know that you are not alone.

It is okay if you are late in starting your journey to improve your self-advocacy skills; you just need to commit to moving forward.

Challenging implicit or explicit norms can be tough. Each person decides how much they're willing to push the boundary (or where they believe the boundary is).

At work, some norms might be clearly stated, but they can be unfair to you. For example, when companies forbid discussing salaries with other employees, it can lead to lower pay for you. Or when a manager avoids talking about your path to promotion, it might be because they don't want to set clear goals and expectations. Also, if your team lead doesn't explain why others get high-profile projects while you're given maintenance work, it puts the burden on you to speak up. These situations share a common thread. They make it difficult for you to advocate for your needs and go against the usual processes.

Often, the norms that discourage self-advocacy aren't clearly stated. They arise from the deeply ingrained mindset of you and those around you. Being assertive might be perceived as selfish, and sharing your preferences could be seen as taking up too much space. Asking for clarity might be labeled as troublemaking. These unwritten rules can make it challenging to advocate for yourself without facing judgment or negative labels.

The absence of formal preparation also contributes to the difficulty of normalizing self-advocacy. In formal education, we learn skills meant to prepare us for the real world. But how many high schools and colleges include self-advocacy in their curricula? How many teachers share their best tips and tricks for advocating for yourself to achieve success? Why is a class that teaches you how to negotiate your salary, seek a promotion, or find a work-life balance considered less important than studying Biology? These gaps in our education can make it harder for self-advocacy to become a widely accepted and practiced skill.

Once you enter the workplace, it can be challenging to suddenly realize that you lack a crucial skill or haven't developed it enough for career success. It becomes even harder to find ways to train yourself in the missing skill of self-advocacy if you lack mentors or supportive managers willing to guide you in that area.

Learning a whole new set of skills can be daunting and make you feel isolated. But if you've struggled to highlight your own accomplishments, know that you can develop this ability and acquire the necessary tools. It's challenging to learn how to talk about ourselves, especially if we haven't practiced it before. It becomes even more difficult when the people around us don't support or celebrate self-advocacy. However, the consequences of not advocating for yourself can be even more difficult to handle.

I moved to the U.S. alone to attend college in Chicago when I was seventeen years old. It was a whole new country for me, and I didn't have any familiar friends or family here. The education system was entirely different from what I was used to. To add to the challenges, I was assigned a roommate who wasn't very friendly. She preferred to study from 1 am to 5 am, claiming her brain worked best during those hours. Her study routine involved playing Avril Lavigne's music loudly without using headphones, and frequent curses directed at her professors. She insisted on this ritual and suggested I leave the room if I couldn't sleep.

Everyone I talked to found my roommate's behavior strange, but back then, I had limited support to confront the situation strongly. As an international student, I constantly feared the risk of deportation for minor issues, so making a big deal out of it wasn't encouraged. Looking back, if I had taken more time to understand why I hesitated to stand up for myself (and my much-needed sleep) and what fears were reasonable, I might have found a different solution. It was a tough lesson to learn, realizing that my belief in always accommodating others at the expense of my own needs was limiting me. The roommate situation only lasted for one semester, but the lessons I learned from that have stuck with me to this day. I advocate for myself, and I don't take sleep deprivation lightly.

If self-advocacy doesn't come naturally to you, try to figure out why. Once you understand those underlying reasons, you can create an action plan to address them methodically. You can also learn from others who faced similar hesitations but managed to overcome them. It becomes much easier to advocate for yourself when you know what's been holding you back in the first place.

Over the years, I've had many conversations with different people, and a few common reasons for struggling with self-advocacy have resonated with me a lot.

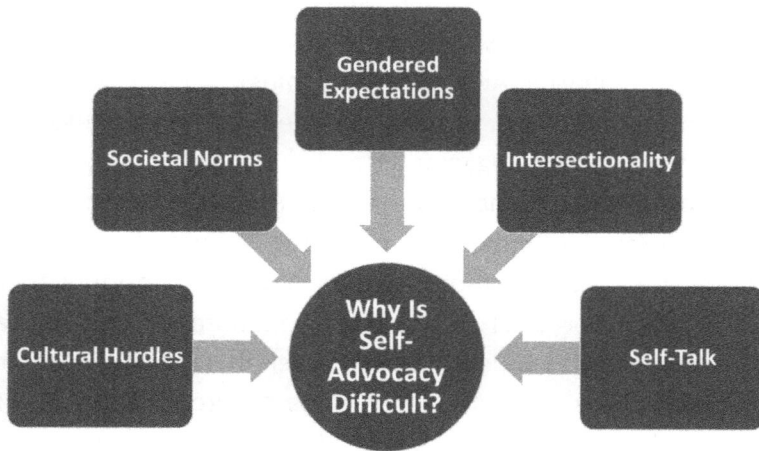

Cultural Hurdles

In numerous cultures, the idea of self-advocacy isn't well understood or valued. It is commonly accepted that boasting, showing off, selfishness, and being demanding are deeply negative traits. Any behavior that even remotely resembles these traits is strongly frowned upon.

Humility is highly valued in many religions and cultures, and it serves a good purpose. If everyone only focused on their own needs, it would be difficult to accomplish things for the greater good of society. No culture wants to prioritize individuals at the expense of the common good. Solely prioritizing individual needs can hinder progress and innovation for the entire community. People have various specific needs that might not apply to everyone, but being humble and acknowledging your needs doesn't conflict with this collective mindset.

Maintaining a low profile is also a common cultural norm. Drawing attention to your achievements or needs might lead to unintended consequences. This trait is often seen in many former colonies, where displaying abundance attracted violence and exploitation. To avoid repeating history, some prefer to keep their achievements private and find their own ways to utilize their talents effectively. However, this approach comes with a risk. Not sharing common knowledge that others have collected can lead to wasting time reinventing the wheel. Balancing the need to protect against exploitation with the benefits of sharing unique skills and finding support to amplify impact is crucial.

Many religions and cultures also value the importance of giving back and serving others, and this is a positive aspect. Giving back is crucial for society's progress, as civilizations have advanced through collaboration, sharing, and supporting neighbors in need. Prioritizing service means actively seeking opportunities to be there for others. However, it shouldn't discourage anyone from expressing their own needs. Your needs are not insignificant just because someone else might be facing greater hardships. The mindset of "don't complain about your missing roof because someone else doesn't even have food" is not logical. Roof and food are not interchangeable resources, and they don't compete with each other. It's possible that someone may have a spare roof to share, and another person might have spare food to share. Your needs are still valid and deserve consideration.

Cultures can be classified as either "collective" or "individual."[1] Individual cultures tend to prioritize the rights and needs of individuals, whereas collective cultures focus on the needs of the group. These cultural differences become deeply ingrained in how people who grew up in these cultures think and talk about themselves. I come from a collective culture where harmony is highly valued, even if it means sacrificing individual well-being. Common phrases include:

- "Just go along with what everyone wants."
- "Don't make a scene and follow what they say."
- "It doesn't matter what *you* want. The entire group wants this."

---

[1] Fatehi, K., Priestley, J. L., & Taasoobshirazi, G. (2020). The expanded view of individualism and collectivism: One, two, or four dimensions? International Journal of Cross Cultural Management, 20(1), 7–24. https://doi.org/10.1177/1470595820913077

In a collective society, harmony is valued because resolving conflicts can be costly and disruptive to the group's stability. However, for individuals, sub-optimal resolutions can have significant costs. Their lives, mental health, and relationships with others can all be impacted by how their individual concerns are addressed. This isn't beneficial for the collective either, as having a group of unhappy and resentful individuals won't contribute to overall happiness in the long run.

In a company where I worked previously, we frequently discussed these topics in our Employee Resource Group (ERG) for Asian employees. During our conversations, we shared numerous examples of how our cultural identity sometimes made it difficult for us to express our needs comfortably in everyday situations. Many phrases were repeatedly mentioned as norms that were deeply ingrained, making self-advocacy more challenging for some of us.

One colleague shared a story of not wanting to take time off while his father was seriously ill because he didn't want to burden his colleagues with extra work. Instead, he worked during the day and stayed up all night taking care of his father. Another colleague faced a toxic and unsupportive boss but hesitated to seek a different situation due to feeling disloyal and ungrateful for being hired years ago. Many people also mentioned feeling uncomfortable with company events or deadlines scheduled on major cultural and religious holidays, but they felt reluctant to say no as they didn't want to appear as though they required too much accommodation. These stories highlighted how cultural norms and beliefs can make self-advocacy challenging in various workplace situations.

Cultural norms should ideally bring joy, strength, and a sense of community. However, when they become obstacles that hinder your peace of mind or restrict your career growth, they no longer fulfill their original purpose. It's important to recognize and address such limitations to ensure that cultural norms positively contribute to your well-being and personal development.

Societal Norms

Social norms often discourage self-promotion or anything that appears flashy or excessive. We are taught to dismiss sales calls and find it bothersome when someone brags about their abilities. There's an ingrained belief that positive words only hold weight if someone else says them about us. As a result, we may downplay our own accomplishments and be hesitant to speak positively about ourselves.

The advertising industry heavily relies on celebrity endorsements to convince us that a product is excellent. Instead of showing us data and scientific proof, many ads feature attractive celebrities enjoying the product to persuade us of its quality. Even in promotional advertisements, we prefer to see someone else praising the product rather than the product itself telling us how great it is. The power of celebrity influence often outweighs straightforward product claims in capturing our attention and trust.

This mindset extends to the workplace, creating a culture where employees often wait for others to praise their work rather than speak up about their own positive achievements. People seek out others who can help amplify their accomplishments, such as their bosses, peers, or collaborators. However, it is not the norm for individuals to proactively write a document or announce in a company-wide meeting about their own contributions that led to positive business outcomes. Self-promotion is not commonly practiced, and employees tend to rely on others to recognize and acknowledge their achievements.

Most people find it easier to highlight the importance of their work in structured settings where it's expected, such as during performance reviews, project status updates, or scheduled sharing of successes. However, not all companies or teams have these structured settings, or the existing formats may not be effective. Even when the format is effective, some individuals may still feel uncomfortable participating and promoting their achievements.

In companies where self-promotion is valued, individuals who excel at it often receive more opportunities, leading to a cycle where they have even more chances to promote themselves. Unfortunately, this cycle doesn't prompt a reset of norms to support those who do great work but may not be as skilled in self-promotion. As a result, individuals who are not adept at talking about their accomplishments may miss out on training or intentional reminders that it's okay for them to advocate for themselves and their work.

The way we expect individuals to behave doesn't always align with what we do at a group level. In many organizations, understanding the needs of customers or constituents is not only extremely valuable, it is often a non-starter for important projects. In Silicon Valley, where I work, it's common practice to gather feedback and suggestions from individual customers before finalizing a product roadmap. Understanding their needs and problems is crucial for solving their issues effectively. Even governments use similar methods by surveying people, inviting individuals to policy meetings to share opinions, and holding polls for direction on what the public wants. In some companies, senior leadership draws inspiration from specific conversations with target customers that drive their passion to address certain areas.

Policies sometimes mention the names of individuals who played a crucial role in explaining why a specific problem was personally significant to them. In those instances, those individuals chose to advocate for themselves with someone influential, and their input helped create solutions that benefited many others facing the same issues but lacked a voice.

When we observe our society and the individuals we admire as heroes, many of their stories revolve around breaking norms and pursuing worthy goals. Students who prioritize fighting for the climate over schoolwork are advocating for their needs. Actors who strive for prize-winning performances in their 50s are prioritizing their aspirations and inspiring others to do the same. CEOs who pursue audacious technology goals and achieve remarkable results are pushing the boundaries of what is possible.

Societies constantly evolve, and the needs of their people evolve along with them. Changing the established ways can be a slow and challenging process, and sometimes change doesn't happen quickly enough to solve your problems. However, every moment spent advocating for yourself serves a purpose in reshaping the way others think. It helps improve the understanding of individual needs. And that is a cause worth fighting for.

Gendered Expectations

Women and marginalized genders have faced a challenging journey to gain visibility and recognition in the workplace. Initially, we fought for the right to have a seat at the table. However, we soon realized that merely sitting at the table was not enough. The real privilege lies in actively participating and having our voices heard during the discussions. But our aim goes beyond that. Being the one who creates the table, sets the agenda, and invites people to participate is the ultimate goal.

Many women receive direct or indirect feedback to avoid being too outspoken. This advice might come from our mothers, who worry about our safety when we draw attention to ourselves. It can also come from our coworkers, who have observed that speaking out can have negative consequences. Even our superiors at work, due to years of a status quo that was predominantly male, might listen more attentively to a man's ideas while scrutinizing or being overly critical when a woman speaks up. All of these and other ingrained behaviors often lead women to become hesitant and refrain from speaking up when it truly matters.

The training to prioritize being liked rather than being seen as smart or competent begins at an early age for women. Little girls are taught to care about others' opinions, while little boys are encouraged to pursue their desires. The toys marketed to girls often emphasize nurturing, while toys for boys focus on building strategy and motor skills. Parents of girls often want their children to be perceived as nice, while parents of boys are more concerned with their intelligence. These early reinforcements lead women to continue valuing being liked as adults while being considered smart is seen as a bonus. This bias is supported by data from various studies on the big five personality tests, where women, on average, score higher on the agreeableness quotient.

In the workplace, this mindset leads to decisions that prioritize getting along with our bosses and coworkers over advancing our careers. When we take on additional responsibilities without any extra incentives, solely relying on a coworker's gratitude, we are choosing to be liked over achieving success. This can lead to burnout without significant rewards and can cause us to miss out on better opportunities. Women often find themselves assigned or volunteering for tasks considered "housekeeping," such as note-taking, organizing team events, or handling mental loads like remembering dietary preferences when ordering lunch. Even tasks that may seem technical, like creating coding documentation standards, can be undervalued compared to tasks that directly impact business profits. These choices might be seen as less promotion-worthy, reinforcing the bias in the workplace.

In the workplace, there is a distinction between "promotable" work and "unpromotable" work, but this difference isn't always clearly communicated. Women are often led to believe that doing enough "unpromotable" work is sufficient and something to aim for. Even when women do get promoted, their success stories tend to highlight their abilities as "amazing champions" rather than "smart superstars." This perpetuates gendered expectations at work, where women become more focused on how they are perceived rather than being intentional about self-advocacy, which does a disservice to their career growth.

When I first entered the industry, I felt grateful just to be included and accepted. People told me it was a privilege to be part of the "cool kids table," so I didn't want to draw too much attention to myself or insist on my ideas being heard. Back then, I was the only female engineer among twelve team members, and also the most junior. Taking their advice seemed like a wise move. However, as I moved on to different teams and situations, I realized how much my voice mattered in shaping my own growth. Looking back, I now recognize several missed opportunities where I should have advocated for myself and challenged the status quo.

Intersectionality

Intersectionality is a term created by Kimberlé Crenshaw in the late 1980s.[2] In her popular 2016 TED talk, "The Urgency of Intersectionality," she explains how different aspects of a person's identity can lead to compounded discrimination.[3] Simply addressing one part of a person's identity may not fully solve the challenges they face. For instance, the issues faced by women and the issues faced by Black people were well-documented, but unique problems experienced by Black women were not fully recognized. Crenshaw's work has been focused on understanding, acknowledging, and addressing these complex challenges that are greater than the sum of their individual parts.

Crenshaw's talk sparked extensive research on the topic, resulting in the generation of numerous data points that were previously lacking. This increased research and data have significantly improved our understanding of the compounding effects she highlighted.

The compounding effects also apply to the reasons that make self-advocacy challenging. As a woman, you may have been taught not to appear too assertive. As a person of color in a predominantly white society, you may hesitate to draw more attention to yourself. If you are a woman of color, both of these factors may be relevant. These reasons can compound, intensifying their impact on self-advocacy.

I've had extensive experience in the health and fitness industry, and there are many instances that illustrate the challenges of self-advocacy, especially for individuals with compounded identities. Women often

---

[2] Crenshaw, Kimberlé. *On Intersectionality Essential Writings*. New Press, 2022.
[3] Crenshaw, Kimberlé. "The Urgency of Intersectionality." TED. TEDWomen, Oct. 2016, San Francisco, CA, Yerba Buena Center for the Arts, https://www.ted.com/talks/kimberle_crenshaw_the_urgency_of_inters ectionality?language=en. Accessed 11 Aug. 2023.

Intersectionality Concepts

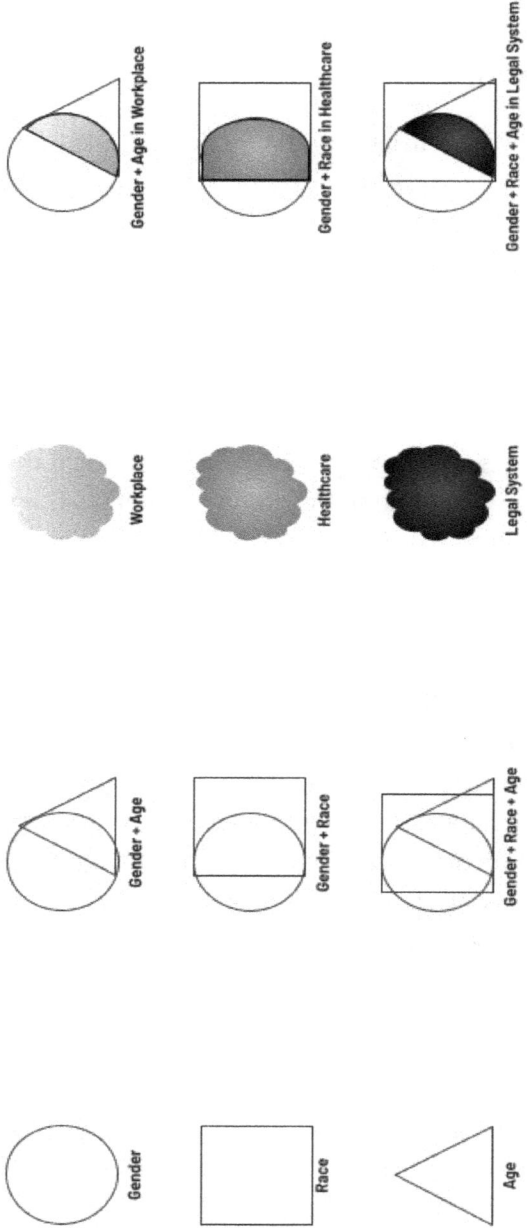

Shapes
Problems faced by an **identity**

○ Gender

□ Race

△ Age

Overlaps
Problems faced by
intersectional identities *

Gender + Age

Gender + Race

Gender + Race + Age

Colors
Spaces in which
problems can be faced *

Workplace

Healthcare

Legal System

Colored overlaps
Spaces where problems are faced by
intersectional identities *

Gender + Age in Workplace

Gender + Race in Healthcare

Gender + Race + Age in Legal System

* Not an exhaustive list

struggle to have their pain taken seriously by medical professionals, and this difficulty is even more pronounced for Black women, as evident in their high maternal mortality rates in the US. The intersection of gender and race can lead to significantly worse experiences for some individuals. Even renowned athletes like Serena Williams have faced challenges in advocating for themselves. Serena shared her story of having to fight for proper medical care after her first pregnancy, as medical professionals initially dismissed her symptoms.[4] Her self-advocacy saved her from dire consequences. Sadly, such stories are not uncommon. While it's unfortunate that self-advocacy is necessary, it's fortunate that some people can effectively get what they need.

For individuals who belong to multiple, intersectional, underrepresented groups in the workplace, it's common to feel hesitant about drawing attention to their needs or achievements. While some people may find it easier, others need to put in effort and practice. A useful starting point is to understand the various identities and belief systems that make self-advocacy challenging for you.

Self-Talk

We are often comfortable answering certain questions on the spot, like where we are from, our occupation, or our food preferences. These questions are easy to handle because they involve sharing factual information rather than personal opinions. The ease also comes from their common use as ice-breakers in conversations. However, when it comes to expressing our own opinions about ourselves, it becomes more challenging. We find it easier to talk about others' opinions or preferences than to openly share our own.

---

[4] Williams, Serena. "Serena Williams: What My Life-Threatening Experience Taught Me about Giving Birth." *CNN*, Cable News Network, 20 Feb. 2018, www.cnn.com/2018/02/20/opinions/protect-mother-pregnancy-williams-opinion/index.html.

In professional interviews, some of the most dreaded questions are the ones that ask about our strengths, professional successes, and the value we bring to our roles. These questions can be challenging because even if we know the answers, it's hard to present them in an authentic manner. Many of us are taught to let others praise us while we remain modest or downplay our achievements. Our self-talk triggers doubts, like questioning whether it's genuine to praise ourselves or worrying if the listener will be put off by us saying we're good. These concerns may make it difficult to confidently express our accomplishments.

During performance review season, many employees struggle to complete their self-reviews. These self-reviews were designed to give employees a chance to share their perspectives on their performance, which would then be discussed with their managers. However, some employees may feel hesitant to highlight all their relevant achievements. They might be shy, take their accomplishments for granted, or assume that their manager is already aware of their successes. As a result, the self-reviews may not fully capture all the important contributions an employee has made. Many people know at some level that if their best friend or sibling were writing the performance review on their behalf, they would use a much more positive tone and hype their achievements a lot more. More people should channel that voice of a loved one for themselves!

As our systems evolve to empower employees to take control of their careers, it's crucial for our self-talk to evolve too. As an experienced manager, I find it essential to remind all of you to seize these chances to speak positively about yourselves. Embrace self-advocacy as a powerful tool to showcase your strengths and accomplishments. Don't shy away from sharing your successes, skills, and contributions with confidence. Every time at work you have an opportunity to share your progress, first remind yourself:

Be kind to yourself. Be proud of your achievements.

You are not inconveniencing anyone by advocating for yourself.

What's Holding You Back?

In the end, no matter what the reasons are that lead to difficulty in self-advocacy, the outcome is the same: a potential hindrance to your career growth. However, understanding the underlying factors can significantly help you tackle this challenge and find the right tools to overcome it. If cultural influences are at play, seeking coaching and appropriate context can be beneficial. On the other hand, if gender-related factors are causing obstacles, there are specific tools available to help you develop those aspects and build your self-advocacy skills. By recognizing the root causes, you can take targeted steps towards becoming a more effective advocate for yourself and your career.

From the list below, which items have you heard repeatedly or even internalized?

- ☐ You should be seen first, heard later.
- ☐ The only thing that matters is that you are a nice person.
- ☐ Think twice before inconveniencing someone by asking for something.
- ☐ Men don't date smart girls.
- ☐ People who praise themselves can't be trusted.
- ☐ Nobody likes a show-off.
- ☐ You should wait for someone else to praise you.
- ☐ Do your work and eventually someone will see how good you are at it.
- ☐ Don't say, show.
- ☐ Be patient and wait for your turn to shine.

- [ ] Don't make too many demands.
- [ ] Asking for things might make them take away what you already have.
- [ ] Keep your head down and don't draw attention to yourself.
- [ ] Being good at things can attract envy.
- [ ] There's such a thing as being too ambitious.
- [ ] You're in a technical career; you don't need to talk like a salesperson.
- [ ] Your boss is busy, they don't want to hear about your needs.
- [ ] Your company will function without you, be grateful that you have a job.
- [ ] Your work will speak for itself.
- [ ] Women care more about the needs of others than their own.
- [ ] In our culture, we are very accepting of whatever life gives us.
- [ ] Don't complain, just accept the situation.

Did you connect with any of these statements? Some of them can be reasonable in certain situations. However, if you find that these statements dominate your inner thoughts, it could be the reason why you struggle to speak up for yourself. Dig deeper into what hinders you from self-advocacy, as a way to come up with an action plan to address those reasons.

Chapter 3
Why Is Self-Advocacy Important?

Advocating for yourself is like making an investment in your career. And investing in your career is one of the most valuable things you can do for yourself. Because when you prioritize your career, all the effort and time you put into it becomes truly meaningful.

We have to be comfortable, confident, and genuine in advocating for ourselves.

For many of us, our careers play a crucial role in our adult lives. Our careers can affect our health, financial stability, where we live, and the people we interact with. It's important to develop the skills that enable us to have more control over our career path. Relying solely on others to manage our careers can be risky, as even well-meaning bosses or supervisors prioritize their own interests.

Throughout our life and education, we receive advice and training to prepare us for successful careers. We learn technical skills relevant to specific jobs, generic skills related to professionalism, and soft skills for working with others. However, self-advocacy skills are often overlooked. How many classes in college taught you how to negotiate your first salary, a raise, or a promotion? While there may be resume reviews and interview training, daily advocacy skills needed once you start a job are often not covered.

These skills are all essential, but most of us don't receive formal training in them. We aren't born with a natural ability for marketing ourselves or advocating for fairness. It can be painful when we know we deserve a raise but struggle to ask for it. Similarly, we may be aware that sharing our accomplishments could lead to a promotion, but we don't know how to present it effectively. Salary negotiations have far-reaching implications beyond just the base pay, impacting bonuses, 401(k) matching, and equity. So why do we find it difficult to excel during these negotiations?

Developing the skills that make these tasks easier demands dedication and commitment. We must remind ourselves of our true worth and refuse to settle for less. It requires putting in the effort to build the necessary abilities so we can achieve the best possible results in our careers. It is similar to how runners who train for a marathon start months in advance with short sprints.

Even if advocating for yourself doesn't come naturally, it's crucial to acquire those skills. Learning to advocate for yourself is like a preventive measure. When you find yourself in a situation where you need those tools, you'll really need them. High-pressure and high-stakes scenarios don't allow for learning something new on the spot. Being prepared with these skills can make a significant difference in such situations.

It is much easier to practice and build those skills along the way, so that you are comfortable with proactive self-advocacy, and are set up for success with reactive self-advocacy.

Self-Advocacy Benefits You

The main advantage of self-advocacy skills is for yourself. Speaking up for your best interests can directly impact your life in a positive way in many situations.

Success in the workplace typically depends on three key areas, all of which can be enhanced through persistent self-advocacy.

Workplace Success	**=**	Developing the right skills	**+**	Landing key outcomes	**+**	Owning your growth path

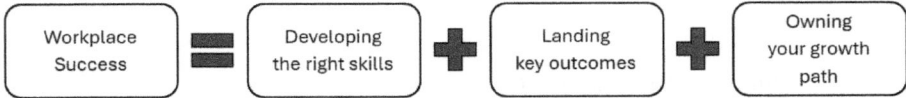

Developing the Right Skills

Acquiring the necessary skills encompasses both technical and job-specific abilities. Additionally, it involves cultivating the right attitude, such as **confidence**, self-awareness, and **authenticity** in your workplace endeavors. While confidence in your qualifications may seem fundamental, this "skill" is often underdeveloped. Self-awareness allows you to honestly assess and improve upon areas that need attention. Being authentic ensures that your work and contributions are in harmony with your true self.

Landing Key Outcomes

Achieving significant outcomes is subjective, and what is considered 'key' can differ from one individual to another. For some, it may revolve around everyday achievements, like completing a project, leading a successful meeting, or mastering a crucial skill. Others may focus on less frequent milestones, such as **negotiating a salary**, **securing a raise**, or **earning a promotion**.

Owning Your Growth Path

Taking charge of your growth path involves proactively managing factors that contribute to learning and career advancement. Acquiring new skills and gaining exposure to diverse experiences positively impact your career trajectory. Securing the necessary **resources** and assistance from the right individuals ensures the sustainability of your career. Long-term **success** in your career often comprises numerous small achievements, many of which can be fully influenced by your actions and decisions.

Confidence

Maintaining a positive and optimistic attitude toward your work and abilities can greatly contribute to your success. When you exude confidence, those around you tend to reflect that confidence too. Projects are more likely to succeed when the team is positive and optimistic about their chances, rather than operating from a place of fear or uncertainty.

Building confidence is not just about using empty tricks; it requires effort to recognize your strengths and areas for improvement. Regularly assessing your skills with honesty has a twofold advantage. First, it helps you identify areas where you can grow, allowing you to create intentional plans for improvement. Second, it reinforces your confidence in the areas where you excel, encouraging you to seek more opportunities to use those skills. This increased inner confidence greatly enhances your chances of achieving your goals. Even if you possess great underlying abilities, lacking confidence can cause you to miss the mark. Confidence is a key factor in realizing your full potential and succeeding in your endeavors.

Engaging in self-advocacy can help you realign your inner mindset and combat imposter syndrome. By confidently recognizing your qualifications and abilities, you can counteract negative or doubtful thoughts that may otherwise distract you. This newfound focus allows you to move forward with determination and assurance, ensuring that you tackle challenges with the self-assurance needed to succeed.

Authenticity

Practicing self-advocacy enables you to pinpoint your genuine desires and requirements. Through the process of self-awareness, you gain a powerful tool for personal growth. Understanding your own satisfaction, needs, and passions empowers you to pursue the right opportunities that align with your goals. With this knowledge, you can present yourself more effectively, knowing that you are pursuing something meaningful and significant to you.

Many individuals dedicate years to pursuing goals they never truly wanted. Sometimes these goals are imposed on them by others, and other times, they don't realize the goal doesn't align with their own motivations. This can lead to feelings of resentment for the time and effort invested in something they don't genuinely care about. Self-advocacy plays a vital role in realigning with your true desires, ensuring that you invest your time in pursuing meaningful goals that resonate with you. By advocating for yourself, you can avoid a life filled with unnecessary regrets and focus on what truly matters to you.

Living an authentic life, where your work aligns with your personal mission, is a true privilege. It is a gift that comes to those who advocate for themselves and actively pursue what they truly desire. By advocating for yourself and going after your goals, you increase the likelihood of finding that alignment and prioritizing contentment in your life. It is through self-advocacy that you can unlock the path to a fulfilling and meaningful journey.

Higher Pay

It's crucial to remember that nobody will pay you more than they believe you're worth, and it's up to you to communicate your value. When you begin a new job, the company is evaluating your potential and trying to understand the benefits of hiring you. Your goal is to showcase your capabilities and potential as clearly as possible during the interview process. By doing so, you increase the chances of securing a starting salary that aligns with your true worth and sets you on the right track for success.

Leaving things to chance is not the way to go. If you possess skills or expertise that are highly valued in the job market, make sure to emphasize them. It's also beneficial to showcase any specialized skills or knowledge that are directly relevant to the position you're seeking. By highlighting these unique strengths, you increase your chances of standing out and securing the opportunities that align with your abilities and interests.

Even if you're already employed, there may come a time when asking for a raise is appropriate, even without a formal promotion. As you work in your role and witness the impact you consistently make, you gain valuable insights to demonstrate the specific value you bring to the table, justifying why you should be compensated fairly.

Small changes in salary can add up tremendously over the years. Back-of-the-envelope math shows that a $5,000 difference at the start of your career can add up to hundreds of thousands of dollars by the time you reach retirement. This demonstrates the enormous impact that early salary negotiations can have.

Self-advocacy plays a vital role in increasing your income and negotiating favorable salaries. By confidently presenting your achievements and worth, you enhance your chances of receiving the recognition and financial rewards that reflect your contributions and abilities.

Job Promotion

Job promotions rely on individuals effectively communicating their value. You must express your worth to the appropriate person at the right time and in the relevant manner. While some may be fortunate and have proactive managers who nominate them for promotions, others may need to take the initiative and explicitly seek a promotion, presenting a compelling case for why it should be awarded to them. By advocating for yourself and showcasing your achievements, you increase the likelihood of being recognized and considered for career advancements.

To secure sponsorship or promotion from a leader, it's essential to consistently remind them of the value you bring to the business. Clear documentation of your efforts and the tangible results they produce is crucial. While a leader may already have positive feelings about your performance, promotions are typically based on explicit outcomes that you have directly contributed to. By providing evidence of your achievements and the impact they have on the organization, you enhance your chances of receiving the recognition and advancement you deserve.

Promotions in the workplace may not always follow a fixed schedule. The pace of career advancement can vary from person to person, and companies may evaluate promotions at different intervals. External factors, such as market conditions, company performance, and team dynamics, can also influence when the right opportunity to seek a promotion presents itself. Being prepared and proactive is crucial for success when the right moment arises. By staying ready and continuously showcasing your value, you can seize the chance to pitch for a well-deserved promotion.

Promotions in the workplace are not solely about advancing in job titles. They can also open doors to new roles, opportunities, and valuable learning experiences that contribute to your overall career success. While promotions often come with a pay increase, the significance goes beyond financial rewards. They serve as a visible recognition of your professional growth, not only in your current position but also in future endeavors. Even if others may not know your exact salary, they can observe your title change and the increased responsibilities you undertake, which can be a powerful testament to your progress and achievements.

Staying attentive to various opportunities for growth and aligning your career path accordingly can be highly beneficial. Learning to confidently advocate for your own career growth can significantly contribute to your success in the long run. By proactively seeking opportunities and advocating for yourself, you can shape your career trajectory and achieve your professional goals more effectively.

Getting Resources

Having the necessary resources can contribute to your job success. These resources may vary depending on your specific needs, such as specialized tools, support from leadership, or collaboration from other teams. Access to learning resources is also valuable, as it can provide solutions to new challenges that you and your colleagues may encounter. Having these resources at your disposal can make tasks easier and enhance your overall performance in your role.

To ensure you have the resources you need for success, you often have to proactively ask for them. Your supervisors may not be aware of your specific needs, so it's essential to communicate clearly about what you require. Many supervisors may not be directly involved in your day-to-day tasks or may not be up-to-date with the current realities of your role. By reminding or explaining to them what resources you need, why they are important, and how fulfilling your request benefits the business, you increase the chances of getting the necessary support and tools.

As a leader of a team or project, you may still need to advocate for resources and support. This includes getting buy-in from peers, superiors, and your team members. It's crucial for everyone involved to understand the value of your project and have confidence in your ability to deliver results. When others see the significance of your work and believe in your capabilities, they are more likely to provide the necessary resources, such as budget, headcount, or talent. Convincing people of the value of your project can also influence their decision to collaborate with you. If they perceive your project as impactful and beneficial to their career, they may be more inclined to work with you and support your efforts.

Effectively communicating the need for resources that facilitate your job can make a significant difference in your success. It's crucial not only to advocate for yourself but also for the teams, tools, and overall situation that contribute to your success. When you can clearly express why these resources are necessary and how they benefit the organization, it increases the likelihood of receiving the support and backing needed to excel in your role. Advocating for a conducive work environment and the tools that enable your productivity can positively impact not only your performance but also the overall success of your projects and the organization as a whole.

Overall Career Success

In essence, achieving success is often contingent on your capacity to communicate your value effectively. The world, in general, lacks the insight and awareness to understand your needs and set you up for success without your active involvement. By advocating for yourself and presenting a compelling case, you make it easier for others to comprehend your perspective and support your goals. Speaking up about your skills and contributions not only garners trust and respect from others but also allows you to have the desired impact on projects and initiatives.

It is through self-advocacy that you can shape your career and ensure that you are on the path to accomplishing your goals.

The foundation of most successful careers lies in individuals knowing their goals and fearlessly pursuing them. When you have a clear vision of what you want to achieve, it becomes simpler to identify the necessary steps to reach your objectives. Moreover, it becomes easier for others to understand how they can support you in your journey. This mutual understanding of your aspirations is immensely valuable since everyone can benefit from any assistance they receive along the way. By being confident and vocal about your ambitions, you increase your chances of achieving your career aspirations with the help of others.

Self-advocacy is not limited to external actions; it also involves an internal commitment. You pledge to prioritize your needs and silence the voice that undermines your worthiness. It motivates you to carve out time for self-reflection, determining your desires, requirements, and opportunities. Leaving life and career to chance is not the best approach;

instead, self-advocacy empowers you to take control and shape your own path, ensuring a more purposeful and fulfilling journey.

Self-Advocacy Benefits Others

Engaging in self-advocacy doesn't only benefit you but also positively impacts those around you. Taking proactive steps to advocate for yourself can pave the way for others who will follow a similar path. On the other hand, reactive self-advocacy can be invaluable to individuals who lack the same privileges and may face challenges when speaking up. By being a role model and standing up for your needs, you can inspire and empower others to do the same, creating a more inclusive and supportive environment for everyone.

Collective Buy-In

In any work you do, collaboration and partnerships are essential. Advocating for your needs, as well as those of your team and department, fosters collective buy-in from others. By openly communicating what is necessary to achieve success and addressing the requirements for collaboration, you establish a shared standard for how work will be carried out and what is needed to accomplish tasks effectively. This promotes a collaborative and supportive work environment, where everyone is on the same page and working towards common goals.

I once had a team member who frequently expressed her frustration about not feeling respected by a partner team, which often presented last-minute requests. During our one-on-one meetings, I encouraged her to think about what could be done to improve the collaboration and how she wanted to address the issue. After some brainstorming, she proposed a solution: she would suggest creating a specific working agreement with the partner team. She drafted some guidelines and shared them with her teammates and members of the partner team to gather feedback. Surprisingly, when there was a genuine effort to find a solution, both teams came up with excellent ideas for what needed to change and how. Acknowledging the problem led to mutual empathy and a shared sense of responsibility. Her self-advocacy for her personal concerns ended up benefiting everyone involved and led to much better outcomes for all!

When individuals advocate for their needs, it can have positive effects for everyone involved. For example, someone requesting new tools can increase efficiency for the entire team. Setting norms for phone-free vacations can prevent burnout and benefit everyone's well-being. Asking for stakeholder expectations to be adjusted based on workload realities can lead to a better understanding across the organization. These advocacy efforts not only benefit the individuals making the requests but also spark important conversations within the group. These discussions help establish new standards that improve the overall experience for everyone, even those who didn't initiate the changes.

Indeed, shaping the shared values of a group that collaborates is a challenging task. Those who step up and advocate for common issues are providing a valuable service to everyone involved. By addressing shared problems, they help foster a more positive and productive work environment for the entire team. This kind of advocacy contributes to a stronger sense of unity and shared purpose, benefiting the collective success of the group.

Prioritization of the End Consumer

Advocating for your needs directly affects the quality of the work you deliver, which in turn benefits the end consumer. When your needs are met, you can focus better, perform at your best, and deliver high-quality products or services. This not only ensures customer satisfaction but also reflects positively on the overall reputation and success of the organization. By prioritizing self-advocacy, you indirectly contribute to creating a better experience for the end users and clients of your work.

In my first job, there was a colleague who was exceptional at creating excellent, well-organized, and well-explained code. Every time I took over a project he had worked on, I was amazed by how little time I needed to understand what the code was doing. His code always had these beautifully neat comments that were clear and straightforward (and sometimes clever). I asked him why he invested so much time in writing the documentation, and he insisted it was for his own benefit, even though the rest of us benefited greatly from it too. He explained that it helped him remember his thought process when he chose a specific solution or tried to recreate something for a different project. The clear result of his dedication to his needs was that it directly benefited our end customers. His high standards raised all of our standards, even though he didn't force us to follow suit. This led to fewer mistakes overall. If someone was absent and something went wrong, any teammate could step in and fix the problem because the documentation made it all understandable. As a team, we were able to create products with fewer errors, resulting in happier customers.

You might suggest improving a process because the current one is slow and takes up a lot of time. By making that improvement, the business becomes more efficient, and you can finish your work faster. Or you might request free coffee at work because it's a nice perk that you enjoy. The happiness you get from this perk can keep you alert and motivated, even in the early morning, leading to fewer mistakes in your work. Another example is when you ask for learning resources and skill development opportunities. These help you grow in your career and become better at your job, which ultimately benefits the customers you serve.

When you speak up for what you need, whether it's to be more efficient or to be happier in your job, the end consumer who uses the product you're building also benefits. Your advocacy leads to better products and services for the consumers, ultimately enhancing their experience.

Creation of a Good Work Culture

When you advocate for yourself, you're also advocating for a better work environment that benefits everyone. By addressing and solving your own challenges, you pave the way for others to have similar problems addressed. This is especially crucial when outdated practices persist and don't align with the current realities anymore. Your advocacy promotes positive change and creates a more inclusive and efficient workplace for all.

My father served as an army officer, and he often had to advocate for himself and our family. Back in the '80s and '90s, it was uncommon for men to take time off work to attend their children's parent-teacher meetings. When he requested such a thing, it caused some commotion. However, over time, his actions influenced his colleagues, and it became more accepted. His superiors recognized the positive impact of job satisfaction and loyalty, which are highly valued in the military. As a result, he was rewarded for his proactive mindset, and the overall work culture benefited greatly from this positive change.

Not everyone can take the risk of speaking up, and that's a common situation. Some requests may be easy and the worst outcome is receiving a "no." However, certain requests can be risky for certain individuals, as they fear negative consequences they cannot afford. For instance, a junior employee in their first job might hesitate to propose a simple process improvement that benefits the business and increases personal satisfaction. On the other hand, you might feel more comfortable bringing it up due to your experience and familiarity with how decision-makers might respond. In many situations, you may find yourself in a privileged position to advocate for important needs that benefit others who lack the influence or access to do so themselves.

Every improvement made for the collective good is also an investment in your work culture and helps establish positive new norms. When we advocate for our needs, we are not just advocating for our own careers, but also for the careers of others. The benefits of self-advocacy can have far-reaching effects that extend beyond what we initially see and comprehend. It's about creating a better environment for everyone and fostering a positive impact that goes beyond the present moment.

Chapter 4
Developing Self-Advocacy Skills

When we have a clear understanding of what something is and why it matters to us, the only obstacle that remains is knowing the necessary tools to achieve it. Fortunately, the skills for improving self-advocacy are easily learnable and practicable – anyone can acquire them!

I divide the process of becoming better at self-advocacy into three parts:

1. Reframing the internal narrative
2. Reframing the external narrative
3. Practicing intentionally and regularly

Reframing how we talk to ourselves internally helps us adopt the right mindset. Reframing how we communicate externally enables us to use the most suitable words or story. Regular practice is what keeps our self-advocacy skills strong and ready to use when needed.

Reframing the Internal Narrative

For many people, the most significant obstacles to self-advocacy come from within. Our mental barriers often prevent us from effectively advocating for ourselves.

Do you find yourself concerned about how others might perceive you if you speak up about your needs? Do you feel uneasy about expressing your requests, fearing that you might be seen as too demanding? Or maybe you find self-promotion to be a burdensome task?

It can be beneficial to jot down the thoughts that cross your mind when you hesitate to advocate for your best interests. Writing it down allows you to better understand those feelings and address them directly. Take a moment to reflect: What were the specific reasons that held you back from advocating for yourself in recent situations?

1. _____

2. _____

3. _____

4. _____

5. _____

What do your answers tell you about why you hesitate? Hopefully, they give you some insight into the themes of what is stopping you from achieving full confidence in going after what you want.

One major challenge for me was feeling uncomfortable about asserting myself and expressing my needs. I had this negative feeling that I might be taking up too much space or attention. When I tried to talk about my needs, I felt like I was putting myself at the center of everything. Similarly, when I wanted to share my achievements in a positive light, I worried that it might seem like I was trying to steal the spotlight. This cultural discomfort of self-promotion made it difficult for me because I was concerned about how others would perceive me.

As I grew older, I noticed how impressed I was with people who could confidently express their needs and have them fulfilled. It was remarkable to see them do it gracefully, and nobody seemed to judge them for it. In fact, in many instances, others reacted positively to their clear self-advocacy! I observed individuals proudly sharing their achievements, and people responded by celebrating their successes. Witnessing these positive examples of self-advocacy from others made me question my own limiting beliefs and reconsider how I approached advocating for myself.

It's fascinating to notice that many people's negative inner voice resembles someone they know. Often, it's someone who held authority or judgment over them, like a parent, family member, teacher, or coworker. However, we have the power to choose whether we want these voices in our head to truly reflect our own thoughts or if they belong to someone else.

Understanding these negative internal narratives that hinder us from advocating for our full potential is advantageous because we can address each reason one by one. If we have common hesitations, a simple online search like "Does asking for a raise make me appear demanding" will provide numerous articles that assure us it does not and offer practical tips on how to do it. There are plenty of freely accessible resources available for various topics that can be truly helpful!

In your network, there are likely many people who can offer assistance as well. Career coaches, trusted friends, mentors who are not your boss, and others who can listen and understand your specific concerns can help you gain a new perspective. It's beneficial to have a diverse mix of people: some more experienced, some at your level, some from your company, some from other companies, and some with similar or different backgrounds. Each of them can provide unique insights and be helpful in various situations. Many individuals are willing and happy to lend a hand if you ask. Building and maintaining these trusted relationships is a wise investment that will pay off when you need support or reassurance.

For some individuals, the industry or role they are in is so unique that it may feel challenging to find others who truly understand the specific problems they face at work. Self-advocacy can vary widely across different industries, and there is no one-size-fits-all approach. Therefore, it's important to focus on building a network of people who are familiar with your niche area. Attend industry-specific events and conferences. Or join professional associations to connect with like-minded professionals. These opportunities can open up many possibilities for gaining insights and support in your specific field.

Sometimes, the internal thoughts that hinder us from self-advocacy can be very specific and personal. For instance, you might feel hesitant to ask for a promotion because your boss is going through a difficult time in their family life, and you don't want to add to their stress. There is a distinction between the general belief of not wanting to inconvenience anyone and the specific situation where you care about a particular person's circumstances. Dealing with each may require different tactics. The key question is whether advocating for what you deserve truly inconveniences someone else, or if it's a story you tell yourself to avoid taking action.

Navigating through this nuance can be empowering. If you determine, through introspection or discussions with trusted individuals, that your promotion is not an inconvenience, you can take steps towards achieving that goal. You can focus on pursuing something beneficial for you, the business (as they retain happy and growing talent), and even your boss (who needs productive employees for effective supervision). While being sensitive to your boss's situation, there are ways to approach these conversations that can ensure positive outcomes for yourself without compromising on their well-being.

Some mental narratives are pretty common, and we can feel stuck in myths that feel true. However, with careful and intentional reframing, we can acknowledge reality. Then we can respond productively.

Myth: *"My talent should speak for itself"*
Reality: Only visible work will be appreciated.

A lot of us have been told that if you do great work, you'll be rewarded for it. Shine brightly and the world notices. But what if nobody is in the same room when you are shining your light?

Over the years, many of the individuals I have mentored expressed their frustration about their hard work going unnoticed. When I inquired about specific examples of the efforts they put in, they often described tasks that were not immediately visible or behind the scenes. For instance, they mentioned activities like bringing misaligned stakeholders together or going above and beyond to complete a project efficiently, ensuring future requests would require less time. While their contributions were commendable, it became apparent that their managers wouldn't automatically know the intricacies of their work without explicit sharing. As a result, it became clear why they were not receiving the recognition they desired and what steps they could take to potentially change that.

Ultimately, people can only acknowledge what they are aware of. It's a common assumption that our skills and talents will naturally be recognized by our leaders. However, it's essential to consider that managers may be overwhelmed with their own responsibilities, making it challenging to keep track of every detail of our work. While they may see that a project has been completed, they might not fully grasp the intricacies and challenges we faced in the process. Therefore, it becomes crucial for us to actively share specific examples of how we add value, ensuring that our efforts and accomplishments don't go unnoticed. By effectively communicating our contributions, we increase the likelihood of receiving the recognition and acknowledgment we deserve.

Intentional visibility is vital because it ensures that the right people recognize the value of your work and the impact you make. When you understand the importance of being visible, it becomes easier to talk about your achievements and contributions. By actively seeking opportunities to showcase your work, share your successes, and communicate the value you bring to the table, you increase the likelihood of gaining the recognition and support you need for your career growth. Remember, advocating for yourself includes making sure others are aware of your skills and accomplishments, setting the stage for a successful and fulfilling career.

Myth: *"Sharing will attract envy."*
Reality: Sharing benefits everyone.

Showing vulnerability can be difficult, especially when you worry that others might judge or envy you. It's a valid concern, and sometimes, it's not entirely baseless.

In highly competitive environments, some people fear that celebrating their success might make them a target for jealousy or criticism. Success can breed envy when opportunities are scarce. However, not sharing success can also have negative repercussions, as it may lead others to assume you're not performing well. Consequently, you might miss out on important opportunities and collaboration projects. Striking a balance between celebrating achievements and being mindful of the competitive dynamics is essential.

A mentee I knew faced a similar situation at work. He excelled at his projects, leading to recognition and praise. However, he realized that he wasn't learning much and was missing out on diverse experiences. To gain access to new opportunities, he had to open up and collaborate with others, allowing them to share in his successes. Even on projects he once did alone, he started involving his team from the beginning, seeking their feedback and ideas. In return, he offered his time to support others in their projects. As a result, the team transformed from a siloed group to a close-knit community. Successes became shared achievements, and instead of envy, everyone embraced learning from each other's accomplishments.

Rather than worrying about envy, consider framing your success as an opportunity to share your learnings and help others improve. Remember that sharing benefits everyone. Don't keep your success a secret, and by being open, you are more likely to learn from others too. Embrace a mindset of collaboration and mutual growth.

People need examples of what worked and what didn't, and if you're authentic in your sharing, it will be beneficial for everyone who hears about it. Share your failures as well. Be the authentic storyteller that people want to hear more from. You'll be surprised how many people appreciate examples of success and focus on what they can take away from it as a positive.

Myth: *"My work is execution, not talking" or "I want to work, not talk about it."*
Reality: Communication is a part of the job.

In some careers, there's an underlying belief that your primary responsibility is to get things done, not to discuss or promote your work. Being skilled at communication can even be viewed negatively in some cases, with the notion that talking is reserved for salespeople and politicians, and everyone else should focus on execution.

I vividly recall experiencing that implicit feeling when I began my career. Occasionally, it became more evident when I mentioned being an engineer, and people expressed confusion, saying, "But you have such great communication skills." It felt like they believed that being an engineer and possessing strong communication abilities couldn't coexist. As someone naturally inclined to be talkative and having a background in debate, it was a challenge to reconcile these two aspects of my identity.

Over time, I came to realize that these two identities don't have to be in conflict. When you examine the metrics of success, you'll notice that communication is a vital part of nearly every job. Sharing knowledge and receiving feedback are integral to accomplishing tasks. If you don't clarify with your stakeholders why certain solutions will or won't work, they won't trust that you're doing your best for them. It's essential for everyone to grasp the depth of your thinking about a problem to feel reassured that you have their best interests at heart. Therefore, take the time to explain why you possess the competence to devise successful solutions.

Another concern is that people often feel that talking about their work takes too much time. I used to think, "I'm an engineer, not a salesperson. They should hire someone else to talk me up." However, the responsibility to advocate for ourselves and explain our capabilities mostly falls on our shoulders. Take, for instance, all the PhDs who spend most of their time deeply involved in research. Eventually, they must present their ideas to the academic community. They can't outsource this task because without effective communication, nobody will buy into their groundbreaking discoveries. Just imagine all the significant innovations we might have lost if the technical minds behind them couldn't find a way to explain their importance to others.

Myth: *"I'm too busy for self-advocacy."*
Reality: Investing in your own growth is always the top priority.

Finding time for even the most important things can be challenging, and this is a common issue, particularly for senior career professionals. With busy schedules and the need to balance work and personal life, it can feel like there are never enough hours in the day. Work itself often demands a lot from us, making it difficult to prioritize self-advocacy, as it may seem like a distraction from other pressing tasks.

Not taking the time for self-advocacy can hold back your personal growth. It's crucial to invest in your growth from an early stage. You never know what the future holds, so developing good habits and processes now can pave the way for the opportunities you want in the future, providing great benefits when you need them.

Many of my friends and colleagues have dreams of starting their own businesses. Some are drawn to the challenges, while others seek the perceived freedom of being their own boss. They don't want someone else telling them what to do, and they want to turn their ideas into reality. However, being your own boss can be tough. Many founders, including myself, found it challenging to maintain a healthy lifestyle, take breaks, and achieve work-life balance. They had not learned to advocate for their needs when they had regular jobs, and now, with every minute dedicated to their goals, it's even harder to prioritize self-advocacy in times of stress. This is a common story shared by people in various situations, finding themselves needing to advocate for themselves in high-pressure moments without having built the necessary skills to do so effectively.

If self-advocacy doesn't come naturally to you, it can be challenging to prioritize learning this new skill, applying it, and seeking change. However, with consistent practice, these skills can become manageable and easier to use over time. Starting early and practicing regularly is key to building up this ability like a muscle until it becomes second nature and doesn't require much thought.

Myth: *"Celebrating wins is flashy & unnecessary."*
Reality: Celebrating wins boosts morale.

Another common mental narrative is that celebrating wins is flashy and unnecessary. Many people feel that it comes across as inauthentic and not essential. Some might be naturally shy, while others simply don't see the value in the process.

Even if celebrating wins doesn't come naturally to you, it's essential to understand that celebrations aren't just for yourself; they benefit everyone around you. Your successes can inspire and motivate colleagues who may be facing challenges in their own work. They provide validation for teammates and anyone else involved in a project, showing that their efforts have contributed to something positive. Often, your success is not solely yours; it could be the result of an entire team's effort, and that calls for celebration.

One of my favorite team activities as a leader was to ask team members to share their "rainbows and clouds of the week." Rainbows were moments worth celebrating, whether from work or personal life, while clouds represented challenges they faced. It was heartening to hear stories of achievements and proud moments, and it often inspired others to share their own celebrations. The activity brought joy and strengthened our team bonds, creating a light and fun atmosphere. Including the challenges also helped normalize the acceptance and celebration of failure. Self-advocacy not only involves showcasing your strengths but also being open to seeking help and learning from the experiences of others.

When you celebrate, you boost the spirits of those around you and create a positive atmosphere. It also benefits you by providing a moment to reflect on your accomplishments and gives you hope for future challenges. Celebrating is like rewarding yourself for a job well done and expressing gratitude for a successful outcome. It's a way of acknowledging the effort you put in and boosting the morale of everyone involved.

Reframing the External Narrative

Even if we are mentally ready to advocate for ourselves and believe it's necessary, finding the right words can be a challenge. We might worry about how we'll be perceived and if our intentions will be clear. For some of us, it can be daunting to figure out where to begin!

It's natural to be concerned about how we present ourselves while advocating for ourselves or sharing our accomplishments. Finding the right words can be challenging, as we strive to stay authentic and genuine. Moreover, effectively communicating our needs to achieve positive outcomes without facing unnecessary negative consequences can be quite difficult.

Sharing Wins

Let's take a simple example to understand how to find the right words. Imagine I have achieved something I'm proud of and want to share it to highlight my skills and accomplishments.

Option 1: Downplay Your Success

> *"The project was **no big deal. Anybody** could have finished it."*

Here is what you'll hear:
- 👍 I finished something.
- 👎 I wasn't the only one who could have finished it.
- 👎 I didn't think the project was anything special.

Here is what you don't hear:
- 👎 I didn't state anything about the complexity I tackled.

👎 I didn't share anything (e.g., a lesson learned or fun fact) that would make you care about it.

👎 I didn't share any tangible results that would anchor you to why this was an accomplishment.

In what you shared, there is one positive statement about your achievement, but also two statements that may not portray you in the best light. On the other hand, there are three (or possibly more) important aspects that you have not included in your communication.

Option 2: Brag about It

> *"I did the **best job** on this project. **Nobody else** could have finished it so quickly!"*

Here is what you'll hear:

👍 I did a great job on something.

👍 I finished it quickly.

👍 I am excited about the project and for me completing it.

Here is what you don't hear:

👎 I feel I did better than others could have done, without explaining why or how.

👎 I didn't state anything about the complexity I tackled.

👎 I didn't share anything (e.g., a lesson learned or fun fact) that would make you care about it.

👎 I didn't share any tangible results that would anchor you on why this was an accomplishment.

Even if one has mixed feelings about the tone and how it may be perceived by the listener, there are still some positive statements highlighting good things about your skills, which is better than the first option. However, there's a lot more left unsaid, which might make the listener doubt what they hear. Facts like "it's finished" or "it took two days" are easier to accept. When superlatives like "I'm the best" or "I'm the fastest" are added, people naturally look for evidence. Without supporting proof or context, they may not fully trust the claims, leaving room for improvement in self-advocacy.

Option 3: The Humblebrag

> *"I **learned a lot** on this **challenging** project, which turned out to be **fun**! I **pushed hard** and was able to **finish** it in **half the time** it was expected to take."*

Here is what you'll hear:
- 👍 I'm willing to learn and grow my skills.
- 👍 I'm open to taking on challenges and not afraid to try.
- 👍 I had fun with my project, maybe next time I can be assigned more such opportunities.
- 👍 I am capable and willing to work hard.
- 👍 I got something that was hard, done.
- 👍 I had a tangible result from it in terms of efficiency.
- 👍 I am willing to talk about my experience doing something.
- 👍 I am excited about the project and for me completing it.

Here is what you don't hear:
- 👍 I'm not relying on negative comparison, to make myself look better.
- 👎 Details

With about twenty additional words compared to my first option, I've expressed a lot more positive aspects! I could add more details, but there's a trade-off in how much to share while presenting initial notes on a win.

I refer to this as a "humble brag" because it's a way of showcasing your achievements while remaining humble. It's a language that those new to self-advocacy can easily learn. However, it's not the only approach, and I don't want to limit your options! The term "humblebrag" is often associated with false modesty or self-deprecation when sharing accomplishments, but I encourage you to focus on the genuine sharing of your successes and be authentic in doing so.

Share Win + Authenticity = Humblebrag

Over the years, I've tried various methods to make sharing my success stories feel natural, and I've also coached and mentored many individuals to find their authentic voice. Sharing tangible wins from my past speaking engagements helped me secure paid speaking opportunities, even before I became a VP or authored a book. Several of my mentees achieved promotions or salary increases after they changed the way they discussed their achievements. Moreover, I've heard from numerous people that talking positively about their work attracted better collaborators who wanted to partner on exciting projects. Learning this skill can bring about significant benefits!

Indeed, there isn't a one-size-fits-all approach to discussing your accomplishments or bringing attention to what's important to you. The example I provided earlier was just one scenario with various options. Your specific situations may differ, and you'll have many considerations and alternatives to explore!

Here are some starting prompts, that can help you find the right words to share your wins:

- What is important or exciting to you about your win?
- What is important to you about sharing your win?
- What do you hope others take away from it about you or your skills?
- What can you hope to teach/share from the story of your win?
- How can the story be interesting to others?

- What are the facts, and what are opinions?
- Why is it important for your professional growth that you share this win?
- How can you anchor your experience as a positive?
- How can you focus on your own achievement, instead of comparisons?

Finding the right words becomes easier when you understand your motivations and consider the specific details you value. While it's beneficial to craft precise messaging, don't overcomplicate it. Simply reflect on your genuine emotions about an accomplishment, and the words will naturally flow. There's no fixed formula for success stories; be authentic and talk about what genuinely matters to you. With practice, you'll become an effective humblebragger in no time!

The last section in this chapter outlines a few more details about how you can practice sharing your wins at a regular cadence.

Asking for What You Need

Sharing a win and asking for what you need are both forms of self-advocacy, but they can feel quite different. When sharing a win, the main challenge might be finding the right words to convey your accomplishment effectively. On the other hand, when asking for what you need, there's an additional fear of potential negative outcomes that you must navigate to ensure a positive response.

Asking for what you need doesn't have to be offensive to the person you're asking. Often, it's just a simple act of sharing your needs. Your needs don't have to take away from others or cause inconvenience. It's not a situation where if you get what you need, someone else loses something important. It's essential to understand these situations and manage the anxiety that might come with asking for what you want, especially when it doesn't harm anyone else.

Even if your request causes inconvenience to someone else, you are not responsible for that inconvenience. It's merely a request, and the possibility of receiving a "no" exists. However, it opens a conversation about how the inconvenience can be minimized and examining what are the overall benefits of fulfilling your request. Your main responsibility as the advocate for your own success is to ask. While it's considerate to address others' inconveniences, if you spend too much time worrying about their comfort at the expense of your own, you're not doing yourself any favors. Treat yourself with the same kindness you would offer a loved one in a comparable situation.

It's also important to consider that asking for something you need might not always yield the desired results. Some individuals might react negatively to being made aware of something they could have done to make things easier for others, even if you're not blaming them. However, this is beyond your control. What you can do is communicate your needs clearly and kindly but understand that it may not always be successful. Regardless of the outcome, the act of asking itself is a valuable learning experience. It helps you understand your own desires and priorities better. It also provides insights into the other person's willingness and ability to help. With each request, successful or not, you become more skilled at asking and more adept at handling future situations.

Asking for What You Need

What:	Why:	Who:	When:	Where:	How:
Focus on What You Need	Explain Why This Is Important to You and Them	Be Clear about Who Plays a Role in Solving Your Need	Consider Acceptable Timelines	The Spaces Where Their Help Matters	How They Can Help You

What: Focus on What You Need

Ensure you are precise and specific when making your request. If there are numerous details, consider providing them in writing as well as verbally. This gives people the opportunity to review and understand the information at their own pace and in a different format.

Writing down your needs can bring clarity and make the process easier. Vague statements like "I want work to be better" lack specificity and actionability. Instead, opt for specific requests like "I want training to improve my coding skills," "I would prefer clearer agendas for our team meetings," or "I'd like to have a flexible schedule on Fridays." If you have multiple needs, prioritize them, and start with the most important ones first.

Why: Explain Why This Is Important to You and Them

When you communicate your needs, providing the reasoning behind them can be beneficial. It allows others to grasp both the logical and emotional aspects of your request. Demonstrating that you've carefully considered the pros and cons also adds value. Clearly state what you stand to gain from the request. Be intentional about highlighting any potential benefits for them or others as well. Even if the positive benefit to them is less immediate, people are more likely to help when they can see the upside for themselves.

Explaining the reasons behind your needs can foster a stronger connection. When others understand that your request supports your well-being, personal growth, or learning opportunities, they become more aware of your priorities. Even if they can't fulfill the specific request, they may think of alternative ways to address your needs.

Who: Be Clear about Who Plays a Role in Solving Your Need

When seeking help, be clear about why you're approaching a particular person, especially if it's not obvious. Differentiate between asking for help because of their capacity to assist, rather than attributing the burden to them. Also, communicate if you've sought help from others.

Approaching managers, superiors, or HR is usually straightforward, since they are responsible for helping employees. However, when reaching out to someone else, explain why they are uniquely positioned to help in your situation. For instance, you might have already approached your manager without success and now seek advice.

Alternatively, if HR lacks familiarity with your specific needs (e.g., if you are a member of an underrepresented group), you may seek support from other allies.

When: Consider Acceptable Timelines

Clearly outline the timeline for resolving your requests, as they usually need timely attention. Include the risks involved for both parties if the issue is not addressed promptly. Providing context about your timeline expectations upfront allows for early feedback on its feasibility.

For instance, you may expect a resolution within a week. If the other party can't consider it for a month, that information is valuable to you. Framing your request around specific events, such as the end of a busy season or the return of a key colleague from vacation, helps your audience understand your timeline better.

Where: The Spaces Where Their Help Matters

Clearly outline if there is a specific forum where their advocacy on your behalf will be necessary. If you don't have access to those forums without their help, it's important to reiterate that. Provide examples and be specific about the options they might have to support you.

For instance, you might need someone to speak up for you in a particular meeting or advocate for you during a specific project. It could also involve a leadership forum that you are not part of, and thus, you need an ally in that setting. Being clear about the context and where you require support helps them understand how they can help you best.

How: How They Can Help You

When asking someone for help, be specific about the actions they can take to support you. Provide clear and flexible guidance, allowing them to suggest preferred options as well. Distinguish whether you seek moral support or a specific action from them.

For instance, if you want them to support your ideas, give them context and details beforehand. If you need their sponsorship for a promotion, let them know what feedback from them would be most impactful. If you seek their assistance in achieving success, explain how you've analyzed your needs and where their help would be valuable. Clarity and specificity will make it easier for them to understand how they can be of assistance.

Indeed, this template shares similarities with storytelling techniques used by journalists. Just like journalists aim to captivate their audience with a compelling narrative, you also hope to convey your needs authentically and effectively through your words. By putting effort into articulating your requests and giving them the best chance of success, you demonstrate a genuine care for your career and personal growth. Embracing this approach can lead to positive outcomes and empower you to advocate for your own success.

Practice Your Self-Advocacy Skills

The most crucial step in improving your self-advocacy is practice. Change how you think about yourself. Practice expressing your needs effectively. Find the right words to share your achievements confidently. Keep advocating for yourself. Keep practicing until it becomes second nature, and you do it without hesitation or fear. The more you practice, the better you'll get at it. Make it a habit, and it will become a natural part of who you are.

Practice in Private

Normalize practicing self-advocacy in private. Do it because you deserve to remind yourself of why you are good at what you do and get comfortable phrasing those words. This way, you can do it without worrying about others' opinions. It's a simple and safe way to start improving. Make this commitment to yourself and take small steps to build your self-advocacy skills.

Some specific things you can try starting today:
1. Document your wins.

2. Outline details about what you need.
3. Put it in a shareable format, even if you're not ready to share yet.
4. Be regular in practicing self-advocacy.

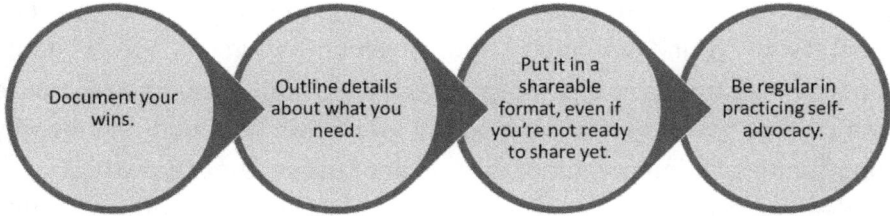

```
[ Document your    ]  →  [ Outline details ]  →  [ Put it in a      ]  →  [ Be regular in    ]
[ wins.            ]     [ about what you  ]     [ shareable        ]     [ practicing self- ]
[                  ]     [ need.           ]     [ format, even if  ]     [ advocacy.        ]
[                  ]     [                 ]     [ you're not ready ]     [                  ]
[                  ]     [                 ]     [ to share yet.    ]     [                  ]
```

Document Your Wins

Make it a habit to journal your wins, either in writing or audio, whichever is more comfortable for you. The format doesn't have to be perfect; the key is to do it regularly!

Each week at work, you achieve something, big or small. It could be completing a project, making progress on complex tasks, resolving conflicts between teams, or setting decision-making criteria. You might have mentored junior colleagues or inspired young talent with your results. No matter the accomplishment, jot it down in your journal.

Documenting the details of your achievements will help you become more comfortable expressing your wins in your own authentic voice. Writing them down is crucial because it forces you to form complete sentences, allowing you to practice using words and tones that feel natural to you. If speaking about your accomplishments is challenging, you can record your voice and listen to yourself praising your achievements. This practice will boost your confidence in self-advocacy.

Being specific about the details in your journal is beneficial. It allows you to refer to your achievements later and helps you remember the nuances. Adding color to why something was important and how you accomplished it will be helpful, especially if you tend to forget those specific details.

Keeping a journal of your achievements is not only helpful for the present but also serves as a reflection exercise. Over time, you can observe patterns in what you choose to write down each week. At the end of the month, you can review your entries and categorize your wins. Are they related to business strategy, interpersonal relationships, or technical accomplishments? By identifying these themes, you can understand your strengths and position yourself for suitable opportunities that leverage those skills. Additionally, you can recognize areas where you may not mention achievements as much and identify opportunities for improvement to facilitate further career growth.

Keeping an honest reflection journal each week can offer valuable insights into yourself and your strengths. More importantly, it serves as a private space for practicing self-advocacy. Writing down your achievements and accomplishments in a voice that feels authentic helps you. It builds the confidence to express yourself and articulate your wins effectively. And when the time comes to share them with others, you're ready.

Outline Details about What You Need

Being self-aware is crucial when it comes to prioritizing self-advocacy. You can't ask for what you want or need if you don't know what will truly make you happy. Taking the time to be intentional about understanding your needs, even if it's just for yourself, is a valuable exercise that should be done regularly.

There are several ways to achieve this. You can create a wish list of items and periodically review it to see how it aligns with your changing needs and track your progress. Another approach is to write freely about how different aspects of your work make you feel, which helps you become more familiar with what you like and don't like. These practices can enhance your self-awareness and aid in self-advocacy.

A structured method to enhance self-awareness is by self-rating yourself on a few important questions, typically one to three questions, every week or so, using the same scale. For instance, you can ask yourself:

1. How satisfied am I with the work I am doing?

2. How satisfied am I with the work environment (such as colleagues, company, manager, and tools)?

Bi-weekly, you can rate your answers to these two questions on a scale of one to five, with five being "very satisfied." Tracking these ratings over time can be beneficial. There might be weeks when work is unsatisfying, but if you consistently rate yourself at low levels (ones and twos), it indicates the need for a change. You can also challenge yourself to answer the question, "What would it take to bring this number to a five?" This encourages you to think about potential solutions. Some of these you can work on independently, while others might require assistance. Reviewing these ratings regularly can remind you to address important concerns and find ways to improve your satisfaction with work and the work environment.

You have the freedom to choose your own questions based on what matters to you. I recommend focusing on areas that you can readily influence, rather than those that evolve slowly, such as compensation. Here are additional suggestions for self-rating questions that you might consider on a regular basis:

1. How satisfied am I with my skill growth?
2. How satisfied am I with the opportunities I am getting at work?
3. How satisfied do I feel with the amount of visibility for myself and my work?
4. How satisfied do I feel about team bonding with my co-workers?
5. Am I having fun doing what I am doing?

These questions can help you gauge your personal growth, opportunities, visibility, workplace relationships, and overall enjoyment in your job. Regularly reviewing and rating these aspects can provide valuable insights and prompt you to act if needed.

Make It Easy to Share (at least, eventually)

As you practice advocating for yourself in private, it's essential to keep in mind that eventually, you will need to share your wins and needs with others. Whether it takes a short time or longer to feel confident, setting the intention early on to "I will advocate for myself in front of other people when it matters" adds purpose to your efforts. Stay mindful of this goal, and as you gain more comfort in self-advocacy, you will be better prepared to share your accomplishments and requests with others when the time is right.

Choosing a regular schedule to refine your notes from their raw format into something presentable is a valuable practice. Whether you write or record your thoughts initially, setting a specific interval to convert them into a format that others can understand is essential. By doing this, you not only hone your inner voice but also develop the skill to communicate your ideas effectively to others. This cadence allows you to share your insights with colleagues, mentors, or anyone else interested in your progress and learnings. It helps you organize your thoughts, add structure to your experiences, and ensure that your message is clear and concise for your audience. Remember, the more you refine and share your experiences, the more you'll improve your self-advocacy skills.

Look out for opportunities where you might share your wins and needs:

- Your weekly one-on-one meeting with your manager
- Your team meeting where people talk about their work
- Your quarterly self-review
- Your promotion case
- Your negotiation for a raise
- A speaking engagement you are applying for
- An award you are nominating yourself for
- An update to your alma mater about what you are working on

There are endless possibilities when it comes to self-advocacy! Having clear ideas about what you want to prioritize can help you focus your energy. By identifying specific areas where you want to improve, you create a roadmap for your self-advocacy journey. For example, you might want to optimize for better communication skills, assertiveness in expressing your needs, or increasing your visibility at work. Having these specific objectives helps you focus your efforts and measure your progress along the way. Remember that self-advocacy is a continuous process, and setting specific goals can make it more manageable and rewarding.

You don't have to share your self-advocacy journey with others until you feel ready, but mentally preparing yourself can boost your confidence. Being ready means you'll feel prepared when the right moment to share arises, even in unexpected hallway conversations. Having your key points and bullet points in mind will help you articulate your needs and accomplishments effectively. Being mentally prepared ensures that when the time comes to advocate for yourself, you can do so with clarity and conviction. It's about being proactive and ready to seize opportunities to speak up for yourself when they present themselves.

Practice Consistently

Consistency is key to your self-advocacy journey, just like when you learned to walk as a baby. It might not feel natural at first, but with practice, you'll get the hang of it. Advocating for yourself can be challenging, especially if it's not something you're used to. But over time, it becomes more comfortable and familiar. Just like learning to walk, you need to be patient with yourself and keep at it. Believe that self-advocacy is beneficial for your growth and well-being, and that understanding will help motivate you to stay consistent in your efforts. Remember, even small steps and regular practice can lead to considerable progress over time.

To develop your self-advocacy skills, set specific goals for how often you want to practice each aspect. Hold yourself accountable by sticking to those goals. For weekly notes on your wins, schedule the time every Friday on your calendar. For regular check-ins on your satisfaction levels, create a recurring task item. And for longer reviews of your notes, set reminders on your phone. Utilize productivity and habit-forming tools to help you stay on track. Practicing with just yourself is essential because it allows you to control the process and reduces the possibility of negative outcomes. Building the habit and skills in this private setting will prepare you to confidently advocate for yourself when the time comes to do so in front of others. Remember, consistency and commitment are key to progress on your self-advocacy journey.

Consistent practice not only improves your self-advocacy skills but also boosts your confidence. It's like building a muscle; the more you exercise it, the stronger it becomes. While you might not need to advocate for yourself right away, the preparation will be invaluable when the time comes. Having the tools and the experience of using them will increase your chances of achieving the desired outcome when you do need to speak up for yourself. So, keep practicing regularly to be well-prepared for any future opportunities that require self-advocacy.

All these exercises lead to one important outcome: you hear your own voice praising and celebrating your accomplishments. Embrace that experience, as it will aid you in the external aspect of self-advocacy. We often struggle to compliment ourselves, but it's time to change that. You deserve to acknowledge and celebrate your wins. You have the right to ask for what you need. It's essential to care about your inner feelings and recognize them, even if only to yourself. So, be kind to yourself and cherish the journey of self-advocacy.

Practice in Public

Practicing self-advocacy in private is an excellent way to begin strengthening this skill, but the ultimate objective is to use it in important public forums. While sharing your accomplishments and needs, most of the time, you'll be doing it with others. Effectively expressing yourself in front of others is crucial for building your career. Remember, careers are often built on people's ability to confidently articulate their goals and aspirations. So, keep practicing, and when the time is right, embrace the opportunity to advocate for yourself in front of others.

All the work you do in private is a crucial part of preparing for public practice. Keeping records and documenting your achievements not only boosts your confidence but also refines your language and communication skills. Self-awareness goes beyond understanding your desires; it helps you brainstorm effective solutions to achieve your desired outcomes. Creating formats that can be easily shared in advance reduces the effort required, especially when time is limited. So, remember that your private practice lays the foundation for effective self-advocacy in public settings.

At a previous job, I was promised a management role in the team, but it took longer than expected because there were no available positions. However, an unexpected chance arose when our team needed to hire a candidate within thirty-six hours. I had already prepared my pitch and process, which I shared with my boss beforehand. As a result, I became the hiring manager for this new role from a pool of internal candidates. It taught me that unexpected opportunities can arise anytime, and being prepared is something within our control!

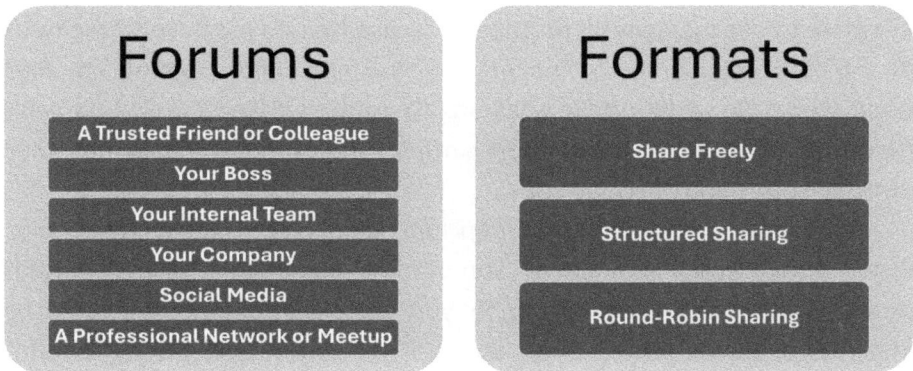

Forums

- A Trusted Friend or Colleague
- Your Boss
- Your Internal Team
- Your Company
- Social Media
- A Professional Network or Meetup

Formats

- Share Freely
- Structured Sharing
- Round-Robin Sharing

Forums for Sharing

When practicing self-advocacy in public, one of the challenges can be determining the appropriate forum. When you have a specific situation to advocate for yourself, the forum is already defined, and you adapt accordingly. However, when you want to practice in a general sense, you may not know which forums are suitable or what formats they allow.

Here are some suggestions for the public forums that could be good places to start:

A Trusted Friend or Colleague

People who know you well and are trustworthy can be excellent practice partners for self-advocacy. You can be open with them about your goal to improve in this area, and if they care about you, they will gladly support you. Practicing your words or role-playing real conversations you plan to have can boost your preparedness. If you trust their judgment, they can offer valuable feedback in a kind manner. You can also reciprocate by creating space for their growth and needs, making it a mutually beneficial exercise.

Your Boss

Your boss plays a crucial role in your career growth and can be a valuable source of support. Keeping them informed about your aspirations and achievements is a smart career strategy. Managers often have regular meetings with their team members, and you can take the initiative to set the agenda for these discussions. Express your desire to share more about your wins and needs, and work together to find dedicated time within these sessions to address these topics and seek feedback. Most bosses will appreciate initiative-taking employees who actively seek such opportunities.

Receiving regular feedback can help you gauge your progress and make adjustments if needed. Sometimes, you might believe certain actions will lead to a promotion, but your boss's input can offer valuable insights. It allows you to pivot sooner if you're not on the right path, ensuring you focus on the actions that genuinely contribute to your career advancement.

Your Internal Team

Your teammates and colleagues can offer valuable feedback and support in your self-advocacy journey. The dynamics within each team range from competitive to collaborative. Within these boundaries, you can find opportunities to practice self-advocacy in a public setting.

For example, during team meetings or daily stand-ups, you can go beyond sharing what you've accomplished and add commentary on why it was significant. Offering your expertise and knowledge can garner recognition for your skills and help the team grow in areas where you excel. Creating a norm where wins and concerns are openly shared can foster a supportive environment, and learning from others' styles can be beneficial.

In some cases, implementing practices like "Gratitude Fridays" can be a terrific way to express appreciation for team members' contributions and highlight areas of expertise. It also encourages a culture of recognition and learning within the team, especially for junior members seeking guidance from experienced colleagues.

Your Company

Your company may offer various forums where you can practice self-advocacy. These could range from company-wide events like all-hands meetings to department-level gatherings or project-specific discussions. There might also be groups centered around specific topics, such as committees or employee resource groups. Keep in mind that not everyone in the audience may be familiar to you, but they are all connected to you in some way.

To build your confidence, start by participating in smaller forums and gradually work your way up to larger ones. Intentionally share information about your work and team's achievements. Don't shy away from bringing up concerns as well, as it can benefit everyone.

If speaking up feels challenging, consider starting with written communication in internal chat or posting forums. As you become more comfortable, you can progress to live interactions or asynchronous methods like emails or surveys. Remember, every step counts in strengthening your self-advocacy skills.

Social Media

Social media platforms are designed for sharing, and the extent of sharing can vary greatly among users. Nowadays, it seems like there are very few restrictions on what can be shared. Rest assured that whatever you decide to share, it is generally acceptable.

LinkedIn is a popular platform for professional sharing, where people commonly post about their achievements, experiences, and challenges. By observing the updates that resonate with you, you can gain insights on what to share and start practicing. The engagement you receive can provide valuable feedback.

Additionally, you can explore other social networks that may have less pressure to share due to their nature or because fewer people you know will see your posts. Platforms like Twitter (if it is still available) might feel like you are talking to the void, but it can be a useful exercise in putting yourself out there and practicing vulnerability. Forums like Reddit or Blind offer anonymity, allowing you to practice sharing without feeling too much pressure.

A Professional Network or Meetup

There are professional networks and meetup groups that cater to various niches. Some may have a broad focus, such as "technology workers in Chicago," while others might be specific, like "product managers in web3 companies." These groups can exist in the physical world or virtually, and some may be tailored to specific demographics. Some are highly active, hosting regular events, while others offer looser connections that you can reach out to when needed.

These networks provide a platform for connecting with like-minded professionals who share similar interests and traits. They can be a valuable resource, as the members are more likely to understand the value of your accomplishments, provide advice for challenges you face, and offer overall support. The more you invest in these spaces, the more you'll gain from them.

Sharing your own experiences and seeking out the stories of others can be incredibly beneficial. These networks have proven invaluable in my career, providing validation for my ideas and introducing me to fresh perspectives I hadn't considered before.

Indeed, exploring additional forums for practicing self-advocacy is a wise step. You can seek suggestions from friends and colleagues who know you well and may offer tailor-made recommendations based on your strengths and interests. Consider joining relevant professional groups, attending industry conferences, participating in workshops, or even contributing to online communities. Each forum may offer unique opportunities to hone your self-advocacy skills and connect with others who share similar passions. The more diverse your practice environments, the more adaptable and confident you'll become in advocating for yourself in various settings.

Self-Advocacy in Action

Once you've identified the forum where you want to practice self-advocacy, consider the formats that align with your style and resonate with others in the group. Here are some suggestions:

Share Freely

In some forums, there might be no specific structure or rules for sharing. You can freely express your wins, challenges, and needs whenever you feel comfortable, with whomever you want to share.

Structured Sharing

If the group prefers more organized discussions, create a norm of structured sharing. You could have designated time during meetings or gatherings where members take turns sharing their achievements, learnings, or concerns.

Round-Robin Sharing

Implement a round-robin format, where each member has an opportunity to speak in a predefined order. This ensures everyone gets a chance to share without any pressure to speak up immediately.

Keep Going

Remember, it's okay to experiment and iterate as you go along. Different forums and days might call for different approaches, and that's perfectly normal. The key is to keep moving forward, taking steps that feel comfortable for you, and gradually building your self-advocacy skills in different situations. With practice, you'll become more adept at effectively expressing your wins, needs, and aspirations.

Engaging in self-advocacy is a crucial step in showing dedication to your path. No matter where you begin, the more determined steps you take, the farther you will travel. Initially, it might feel challenging, but support is readily available, and you can discover the resources necessary for advancement. Your career will benefit from your commitment and effort!

Chapter 5
Creating a Plan for Self-Advocacy

To excel in honing our self-advocacy skills, we must first set clear intentions and then take responsibility for our progress. Without measuring our efforts, we won't be able to gauge our success.

Measuring success in self-improvement can be challenging due to its subjective nature. Yet, breaking down the areas you want to improve, defining your strategies, and tracking your progress can lead to more meaningful advancements. Once you identify your goals, the uncertainty diminishes, and you can navigate your path with clarity.

As someone immersed in the world of data, I often find myself applying these principles to self-improvement. Just like building a software product, I define the desired output and the input metrics needed to achieve it. Then, I assess the actual output metrics, which show what has been accomplished. While it might seem unconventional, this approach works well for our own growth journey. Our mind and body are like products that can be enhanced, made more efficient, and aligned with our innermost desires.

Setting Goals & Measuring Success

You are embarking on a personal journey to enhance your self-advocacy skills. No matter where you begin, the aim is to make strides and advance along this path of self-improvement.

Each person finds unique ways to stay motivated and achieve their goals. For some people, relying on proven methods that work is beneficial. However, if you prefer a structured approach, the framework

I've presented below might be helpful. The key is to enhance your self-advocacy skills, tailoring the process to your preferences. If the framework is effective, embrace it, but don't hesitate to explore other methods that align with your needs.

I propose a step-by-step framework that can help you set goals and track progress:

1. Identify your starting point.
2. Determine your goals.
3. Plan out the path you will take.
4. Commit to a realistic timeline for various milestones.
5. Create a plan to periodically review and iterate.

Identify Your Starting Point

Increasing your self-awareness about where you currently stand on your journey to better self-advocacy is essential. Understanding your starting point allows you to set achievable goals and create a well-thought-out plan for your future actions.

Figure out what phase of self-advocacy you are at now (these are mostly sequential):

Phase 1:   You understand what self-advocacy would look like for you (Chapter 2).

Phase 2:   You understand why self-advocacy is hard for you (Chapter 3).

Phase 3:   You understand why self-advocacy is an important skill for your career (Chapter 4).

Phase 4:   You are able to reframe your mental narrative towards self-advocacy (Chapter 5).

Phase 5:   You have the tools to reframe your external narrative and to advocate for yourself in the right way and have practiced both in private and publicly (Chapter 5).

Phase 6:   You have practiced often, but you are still concerned about landing important milestones (Chapters 8-10).

Take note of your current phase in the self-advocacy journey. You can add a date to easily track your progress. As you move through the phases, review the relevant chapters to support your growth.

It's completely normal to go back and forth through the phases! Our comfort levels evolve, and we may increase what we want from each phase. As we grow and learn, we might also unlearn things that no longer serve us. When unlearning habits that hinder self-advocacy, you can reevaluate which phase to focus on. It's all part of the continuous learning and growth process.

Identify Your Goals

Once you know where you're starting and the phase of self-advocacy development you're currently in, you can set specific goals for yourself. These goals should align with your current phase and focus on what you want to try next to improve your self-advocacy skills.

Creating SMART goals is essential for maximizing the process. SMART stands for Specific, Measurable, Achievable, Relevant, and Time-bound. By framing your goals with these elements in mind, you can ensure they are clear, trackable, realistic, relevant, and have a specific timeline for completion. The concept of SMART goals has governed corporate settings since the early 1980s.[5]

Indeed, goals are highly personal, and it's important to tailor them to your specific needs and preferences. However, learning from others who are also working towards self-improvement can be inspiring and provide valuable insights. By observing their goals, you may discover new and exciting ideas to incorporate into your own journey. Each person's unique perspective can offer a fresh approach to self-advocacy and open doors to growth and development.

If you're having trouble coming up with ideas and need a place to start, I've got a few goals to share below. Keep in mind that the details of

---

[5] Smart Goals: An Acronym for Success - Indeed, www.indeed.com/hire/c/info/smart-goals. Accessed 30 Aug. 2023.

these goals can vary based on your preferences (for example, you could choose a different timeline, a different task to complete, or an entirely different goal altogether). The main thing is to select something that feels right for your current situation. Here are goals to consider based on the phase of self-improvement you are in:

Phase 1: Understanding Self-Advocacy

- Complete the exercise at the end of Chapter 1 of this book and record your score. Over the course of a week, add five new items to the list of situations you may encounter daily. Read books or articles or watch videos from people who explain self-advocacy. Commit to consuming five new pieces of content in the next month.
- Over the next two weeks, talk to at least five friends / colleagues / family members who know you well. Seek suggestions about the type of situations where they often advocate for themselves and where they struggle. Ask them for at least one piece of feedback each on situations where they have seen you do well / not well on self-advocacy.

Phase 2: Identifying Why Self-Advocacy Is Difficult for Me

- Complete the exercise at the end of Chapter 2 of this book and reflect on the phrases that resonated. Reflect on where these mindsets originated for you and see what themes you can identify. Consolidate the top three relevant themes over the next two weeks.
- Over the next month, talk to at least five friends, colleagues, and/or family members who know you well. Ask for stories about why they find or used to find self-advocacy difficult. Record the themes that resonate.

Phase 3: Understanding the Importance of Self-Advocacy in My Career

- Write down a list of things that are important for you to achieve in your career in the next month. Prioritize the top three to five things you really want to prioritize. Reflect on which of those goals require you to self-advocate.
- Think of at least two times in the last year when you missed out on professional success (e.g., didn't get to work on a key project, didn't get a raise or a promotion, or weren't accepted into the college of your choice). For each scenario, brainstorm five ways demonstrating self-advocacy might have changed the outcome of those events.

Phase 4: Reframing My Mental Narrative

- Read the example mental narratives in Chapter 4. Which are the ones that resonate most? Can you think of at least two additional mental narratives hindering you from advocating yourself? Spend two weeks journaling about these limiting beliefs.
- Reframe your top two mental narratives. Ask three friends for help and feedback reframing those narratives.

Phase 5: Reframing My External Narrative

- Look up five recent examples of people sharing their wins from within your organization. Over the next two weeks, write down what you liked about the way they shared their wins (e.g., forum, wording, tone). For each of those examples, rephrase it in a way that resonates with you.
- Write down a list of the top three to five things you want to improve regarding your work environment, team, process, and so on. Over the next month, identify the who, what, why, where, when, and how for that improvement. Document these details in your own words, as if you were creating a proposal.

Phase 5: Practicing in Private

- Commit to keeping a weekly journal to record your top achievements for the next three months. Strive to identify at least two meaningful victories (big or small) each week.
- Over the next month, identify three topics about which you are an expert. Create an article, blog post, or presentation on at least one of those topics.

Phase 5: Practicing in Public

- Twice over the next month, post on your team's chat to share details about a project you did well.
- During a live meeting with your team in the next two weeks, share a recent win and ask others to do the same.
- Within the next two weeks, post on social media (LinkedIn, for example) about a personal victory or professional learning. Talk about what you did, why it was important, and why you are proud of it.
- Over the next month, apply to five conferences to speak on a topic within your areas of expertise.

Phase 6: Planning for a specific milestone

- When did you last get a promotion? Create a list of five tactics that you can deploy in the next 30 days to increase your odds of getting a promotion. Review Chapter 7, read articles, and watch videos to get ideas.
- When did you last get a raise? Come up with a list of five tactics that you can deploy in the next month to increase your odds of getting a raise. Study Chapters 7 and 8, read articles, and watch videos to get ideas.
- Are you happy with your work? Generate a list of five tactics that you can deploy in the next thirty days to increase your happiness

at work. Need ideas? Look at Chapter 10, read articles, and watch videos about creating happiness.

- What other professional milestones are important for you? Over the next month, write down the top three goals you want to optimize for by the end of the year. Create a plan for each item on your list.

These are some examples of goals you can choose, depending on your phase and comfort level. Use them to spark ideas. Make them your own and select the strategies that meet your needs!

Identify the Path You Will Take

There are many ways to get from point A to point B. After you identify your starting point and next goal, your next step is determining how you will make the journey. Everyone has a unique style, and the knowledge of what motivates you is something that only you know. Take some time to explore various ways to create a path tailored to your journey to improved self-advocacy.

Single-Player Mode vs. Community Motivation

Some people like to explore solo and are more than capable of holding themselves accountable. They prefer it. Proving to themselves that they are getting better and are improving at a pace that feels right to them is the most important thing.

Others benefit from a community that shares their general goals. Watching others attempt the same journey can be very motivating. You can learn from others, see what works and what doesn't work for them, and build a community around the fact that you are all trying to get better at similar things.

I worked at Strava (a social network for everyday athletes) as their Head of Data for two years and learned a lot about motivation and habit formation for individuals. It is fascinating to see the differences in what people care about. One person on their self-advocacy journey may care most about tracking consistency and progress. In contrast, somebody else may care most about having that space to celebrate the tiny milestones with others.

While there are no social networks or tools designed explicitly for self-advocacy (that I know of), you can utilize other existing tools for this purpose. Solo players might benefit from the vast landscape of productivity tools that help track habits and measure progress. Community players can benefit from existing social networks (e.g., Facebook or Twitter groups), find communities (e.g., Meetups, WhatsApp), or share their progress with existing connections to build momentum.

Aspirational Targets vs. Easy Wins

For some people, setting a very aspirational target is the best motivation. If you set aspirational targets, expect to fall short of reaching all your goals (since you picked stretch goals). Achieving even 75 percent is a success. Setting aspirational goals also allows you to focus on your vision, the ideal world where you have accomplished all the improvements you wanted to make. That vision can help create intention and alignment. You will make micro-decisions aligned with that big picture rather than keeping your focus on the immediate next step. Doing so allows you to be more flexible as your vision and environment evolve.

For others, aspirational targets less likely to be fully achieved can be demotivating and overwhelming. These people will do much better with setting their intention on easy wins. They can map the path and set milestones that split the effort into simpler chunks. It builds confidence and purpose as they successfully wrap up a portion of the goal. It also allows them to measure progression toward that final goal more quickly. Another advantage of setting easy wins is that you can seek help more easily when even the easy win is hard. Finding the help you need with the little pieces is more straightforward than finding resources to help you tackle a vast goal.

While my husband favors aspirational targets, I prefer easy wins. I derive considerable motivation from saying I want to do something and then checking it off my list once I do it. A big, unchecked goal I've been staring at for weeks is unmotivating. Instead, I like to break down the problem into easy, sequential parts and check tasks off as I go along. My husband, on the other hand, is not even interested if the goal seems too easy. He is motivated by demanding challenges that feel like monumental achievements when accomplished. We have very different styles that work for us individually!

Start Narrow vs. Start Wide

Many people find comfort in knowing they are starting with a reasonable goal. They then have the flexibility to expand their vision as they learn more about the realities of the process. This approach helps reduce the initial noise and gives people a simple starting point rather than choosing from among multiple options.

Others prefer to start with brainstorming and identify how they might tackle a problem. Seeing ideas that, even off the bat, seem pretty wild can be liberating. You'll naturally articulate why the approach is absurd. Perhaps only parts of the concept are unrealistic, and there is value in the rest of the idea.

Deciding your starting point, whether you are going wide or starting narrow, can also be a deeply rooted preference for many folks, and it helps to know your stylistic choice here before you start.

If you have worked in design or with designers, you might be familiar with the double-diamond approach.[6] When solving a problem, you first diverge and broadly consider all the possible options, then narrow them down to a few. The double diamond part is where you diverge first and converge your thinking two times - once when identifying the problem to solve and once while identifying the solution to implement. It could also be an interesting concept to apply while thinking about self-advocacy.

---

[6] Ayre, Jon. "Innovation by Design - Evolving the Double Diamond." *Equal Experts Australia,* 17 Aug. 2022, www.equalexperts.com.au/blog/our-thinking/innovation-by-design-evolving-double-diamond/.

Stick with the Path vs. Feel Out the Moment

Once you identify your journey, it may be easier to plan out the whole path and stick with it until you reach a particular milestone or evaluation point. People with this preference aim only to reevaluate the approach if there is a clear indication that things are not working. They like to spend their time going on a path and only pausing for directions when there is a fork in the road.

For others, a strict path can feel too regimented and may suck the joy out of the journey. They may come on the main street or wander along the sidewalk if that feels right. It is easier for people with this preference to adapt to the path that feels right for the moment rather than trudge along something that may yield a result later. They tend to start on a course with a general idea of where they are going and then decide every day which road they want to take.

Again, there is no correct answer on what style you should choose. Pick the one that works for you! It is better to select the option that helps you reach your goals, regardless of how you get there.

These choices for the path you will take are individual and best chosen after you are honest with yourself about your style. Don't worry if something doesn't work the first time! You can always make tweaks, take a slight detour, or choose a new path that feels better.

Identify a Realistic Timeline

Timelines are essential on any journey. If you have a big lofty goal but need to plan on when you want to see results, you may miss reaching the goal altogether. We are ultimately advocating for ourselves to invest in our success and get better career results. Careers have timelines associated with them!

When you set a goal, time-box it. Setting an end time helps you review your progress at a fixed point in the future. After that, you can reset timelines if you can't hit the first one or examine the scope of what you are trying to accomplish within that time frame.

Doing things consistently and at a regular cadence is also a fantastic way to build momentum. Make a weekly commitment to advocate for your best interest at work (even if it's a small thing). Doing so builds confidence as well as that muscle that makes it easier every single time.

Setting timelines for milestones is something you do individually. There is no correct timeline for when you should have mastered self-advocacy. Even if there were, there is always room to improve! Self-advocacy can be a lifelong journey, and you pick milestones relevant to situations and goals.

Periodically Review and Iterate

To measure success in any self-improvement journey, it helps to create a plan that you periodically review and iterate on. You can't keep going down a long path without measuring success and tracking progress. For all you know, you may have missed a turn you were supposed to take a while back! It is good to orient yourself and review to ensure you are on the intended path and heading toward your goal.

It is also a great idea to iterate and make changes that better suit your needs. Do your goals need to be more challenging? Too hard? Are you getting lost by yourself? Is it overwhelming to hear about other people's progress? Do you need to review your progress more often? Are you getting distracted by reviewing your progress too frequently? It helps to check in with yourself and iterate based on what works best to help you achieve your goals.

Self-Gratitude

Measuring success is a way for you to find confidence in your progress and hold yourself accountable for your journey. The best thing to pair with that is a healthy dose of gratitude for yourself and the journey you have set out on!

Gratitude can be incredibly powerful in reminding us why we are focusing on improving our skills in the first place. Acknowledging the little, positive changes we have already started to notice can embed the feeling that we are pursuing a worthy goal in our subconscious. When it is in our subconscious, it reminds us to do it more often and intentionally.

Expressing gratitude also helps us from feeling discouraged. We don't hit every milestone and goal we set out to achieve. But we are making progress! Sometimes, the improvement can be as little as acknowledging that we want to improve. Sometimes, that progress is that we even care to learn more and keep an open mind about a skill we can develop. Whatever progress means for you, it is good to acknowledge and appreciate it as a reminder that you are still moving forward. It is easy to stay stagnant and never try to change the status quo. It is challenging work to try new things, especially if they are inherently difficult for us.

Find a regular cadence at which you will reserve five minutes in your day to express gratitude. Whether you choose daily, weekly, or monthly does not matter if you stick to the habit. Creating a new routine will be even more effective if you record it somewhere!

Reflect on these questions to build a practice of gratitude:

- What am I doing well in my journey?
- Whose support am I thankful for?
- What tools or resources have accelerated my progress?
- How far have I come from my starting point?
- What have I learned and internalized that has made my life easier?

I believe in thanking the universe for how far we have come. We can use that subconscious message we send ourselves to become even better. If we convince ourselves that we can improve, it will be easier for us to find the psychological energy to seek improvements.

Chapter 6
Helping Others with Self-Advocacy

Why does a book on "self" advocacy have an entire chapter on helping *others* with it? Great question!

Caring for yourself is caring for the needs of others who bring you joy.

Self-advocacy and advocating for others can co-exist. Instead, they are likely to compound each effort. When you help others succeed, they are more likely to help you with your goals. Even if they can't or won't, you still benefit by honing advocacy skills. When you advocate for yourself, you are helping others too. Each example of someone winning by highlighting their accomplishments or asking for what they need makes it much easier for the next person.

"Self" can mean something beyond an individual. It can mean a team, a group, or a community you are a part of. Often, working toward the best interest of that group also helps our own individual best interest. For example, if you attribute some of your challenges to being a woman in tech, then advocating for the needs of all women in tech can help you as well.

Self-advocacy is not a zero-sum game. When advocating for someone (yourself or a group you belong to), you aren't taking something away from someone else. It is important to remember this, as there is often a false narrative that implies some underlying competition. Women's rights and needs in the workplace aren't about diminishing men's rights. Addressing underlying biases against underrepresented groups in the industry won't result in taking jobs away from overrepresented groups. Advocacy is about creating equity and improving outcomes for those who don't have great outcomes right now.

Our best-developed skills are the ones that are always top-of-mind for us. We don't wait for special situations to use these skills. Instead, we are perpetually in that mode. The skill becomes a well-practiced muscle that we are used to, and we almost feel uncomfortable when we don't use it. So, whether that skill is used for our benefit or a purely altruistic purpose doesn't matter.

Using our powers for good to help our community has other benefits. Self-advocacy is hard for many people, and normalizing it also enables us. When proactive or reactive advocacy becomes the norm, we shy away from it less as a society. It almost becomes expected. A great example is how "always negotiate the first salary offer they make" has become such a common mantra for jobseekers that it is no longer taboo. Employers expect candidates to respond with a counteroffer; this is a default expectation in many industries.

Sometimes, seeing what someone else needs and why we must amplify their wins is much easier. With that distance and emotional detachment, sometimes we can see things more clearly. Developing the habit of seeing those situations for others where there is benefit in speaking up can also help attune us to the same thing for ourselves.

As a Leader

Sometimes, it is either explicitly or implicitly a part of your job to help others with self-advocacy. Suppose you are a manager, a team leader, a department head, a coach, a mentor, or anyone in a position of power or influence over someone else. In that case, you can and should be proactive about helping people with self-advocacy. If you care about someone and their career, it is beneficial for you as a leader to put your weight behind this skill. They may have you to watch out for them today, but that might not be true in the future, so you'd instead empower them with the skill and highlight the importance of developing it. You may not struggle with the skill (even if you used to), but you can empathize with and help those who do.

Even if you are not in a leadership role, you may still want to read this section. First, it can help you in the future when you consider those roles. Second, it can help you convince your leader to help you advocate better for yourself.

Why Teach Others This Skill?

Empowered Teams = High Business Impact

There is something in it for you when you, as a leader, empower your team to advocate for themselves!

Businesses do well when people take ownership. Great leaders empower teams and individuals and encourage them to ask for what they need. You want a team that feels invested in the problems they must solve and that can ask for support in solving those tasks. They should know that their job is to be hands-on and to recognize any obstacles to meeting business goals. Remind them that once they point out a blocker, your job is to help "unblock" them. It may not be possible to clear them 100 percent of the time, but it should be regular practice for your team to highlight issues and ask for your help.

Employees who focus on self-advocacy and ask for what they need to do their jobs are more productive than those who do not. It is more efficient for the business to normalize employees highlighting their concerns since a return of investment analysis on addressing those concerns can help pick the mutual wins.

Empowered teams have a more positive impact on the business. A business does well when individual employees act as owners and work efficiently. The best teams I have run were proactive in bringing up concerns, collaborative in looking for solutions, and reasonable in their expectations. Empowerment didn't happen by accident; it happened because I prioritized it. The people in these teams also went on to run highly impactful teams themselves, so the gifts compound!

Diversity and Inclusion

Promoting self-advocacy on your team is also a win for diversity and inclusion. You want everyone on the team to succeed, not just the good talkers.

Self-advocacy may be more challenging for some folks than others, and it has nothing to do with their core professional skills. It's harder for underrepresented groups who don't see successful examples of people who look like them at work or don't want to stand out. It's harder for introverts, who find extensive interactions with people draining. It's harder for people who are shy, who don't know where to start, and worry about how they will come across. They may still be fantastic engineers, marketers, or designers, and their lack of self-advocacy skills should not hinder their success.

Only certain people on the team are comfortable asking for what they need. Only some people are good at highlighting their work. As a leader, you must work harder with people who struggle with it. It is your responsibility to help them have the right tools they need to succeed. It helps a diverse team thrive, not just those from a single mold.

Underrepresented groups often feel like they don't belong, and they may feel pressured to conform and not ask for what they need. As a leader, you are responsible for intentionally making employees feel psychologically safe in bringing up concerns. That psychological safety increases their trust in you as a leader and goes a long way in making them feel included.

Risk Reduction

Promoting self-advocacy on your team is a tactic for risk reduction. If people aren't comfortable telling you what they need, or they don't feel celebrated, they won't like working with you for too long. It is common knowledge now that most employees resign because they want to leave their managers; they aren't vacating their roles or the company as often. If they have other more appealing options—where they feel they'd have to advocate for their needs less, feel more celebrated, or feel heard, their incentive to stay in the current situation declines.

Lack of self-advocacy also leads to resentment. If you have a teammate who doesn't have the tools to shine a light on their achievements but gets upset when their flashy coworker gets a shout-out from the CEO, it still becomes your problem. They may miss out on things they care about because of their underdeveloped self-advocacy skills. They may also miss out on resources or solutions because they don't know how to ask. Watching others get those things can be painful, and if they haven't even shared it with you, you may not realize their resentment is growing.

Inefficiency is another by-product of underdeveloped self-advocacy. If people on your team are not asking for things that make their life easier, their lives will be more difficult. They will take longer to reach objectives. It's terrible for them and their satisfaction levels, and it isn't good for the business!

I have left multiple jobs because of reasons like these. In some cases, earlier in my career, I couldn't advocate for myself because I didn't know how or understand why. In other instances, I advocated for myself but didn't get the right results. The skill was new for me, and I was unpracticed. There were likely also specific nuances that I needed to include to make my self-advocacy "acceptable," which were different for my colleagues who didn't look like me. My direct manager didn't support my self-advocacy proactively or reactively, even if I liked working for them. That ultimately led to my departure, which was good for me (I left for considerably better jobs each time) but not great for the business (they lost a consistently high performer each time).

When people don't verbalize their needs, you miss opportunities to help. You may have unnecessary attrition because someone was uncomfortable asking for a raise, a raise that you could have easily given them. People may have other blockers that are easy fixes for you as a leader. If they don't ask or even know they *can* ask for those resources, it is harder for you to solve those problems for them.

Actions for Leaders

Help Your Team Develop the Core Skills

As a leader, you are uniquely positioned to support and grow the careers of those who work with you. If you manage a team, you are responsible for the growth and career development of the people who report to you. You help them set their goals and identify the skills they need to develop. When you notice people whose careers stall from their lack of developed self-advocacy, it helps to be proactive with them about developing those core skills.

Ask them explicitly about things they need to do their job well and share the challenges they face with you. Normalizing this by asking them instead of waiting for them to bring it up themselves helps them build the self-advocacy muscle. It forces them to think about what they want and what they need. Find a regular cadence during which you ask them to share what they are proud of working on. Don't wait for the performance review cycle to kick in. When employees feel supported by leaders in sharing these things, they feel more empowered and get more comfortable doing it. They expect from you a space where they can highlight their achievements, and eventually, they get better at sharing them.

Some of my best managers have been the ones who normalized my self-advocacy and even praised it. Some even offered specific suggestions for improvement, such as reframing a win in a voice that felt natural and escalating concerns up the chain. Over the years, I've spoken to and mentored hundreds of people. Many have mentioned how important it is when leaders support their self-advocacy journey and how much their careers improve. One lady I met years ago shared that she loved her boss and would follow them anywhere. Her favorite part about them? They always corrected her whenever she talked about herself in the slightest negative voice. The endless cheerleading her manager did was invaluable to her.

Remind Your Team of Situations Where They Need Self-Advocacy

Many people, especially those closer to the start of their careers, don't always see the value of developing skills for self-advocacy. It is not a skill we learn in school or college, nor is it regularly highlighted. Perhaps negotiating a salary is the most common thing people might be aware of. But succeeding in your career goes beyond a fair wage and specific high-value moments.

If you mentor, manage, or coach someone, highlight the routine moments in their career where self-advocacy skills will be crucial. Help them understand why that meeting they attend weekly with all their teammates is not just something they need to get through but a great forum for them to highlight their work and needs. When they tell you stories about work-related frustrations, guide them to leverage their self-advocacy skills to get what they want. Specific examples of situations and career moments relevant to the individual are always beneficial. When you share details about your journey, and those include relatable examples where you did or didn't (but wished you did!) advocate for yourself, it can be powerful.

At a previous company, I was new on the team and presented to very senior executives. The company style and processes were quite different from what I was used to and way more formal. My style remained quirky but engaging, eliciting a positive result. My then-boss had seen that difference already and saw my nervousness about adapting my style to the new situation. He proactively said, "Let your personality shine. You're great at your job, and you don't need to cater to the norm excessively," That advice went a long way for me in my career since it helped me seek out situations that were a better fit for me instead of just focusing on fitting in. It was also a great reminder that I had unique things to offer, and suppressing those pieces wasn't in the business's best interest either!

Actively Sponsor Your Team

If I had a penny for every time I saw a well-intentioned leader offer to mentor, coach, or advise someone but make zero effort to sponsor them actively ... Well, I'd have a lot of pennies! Active sponsorship requires putting your time, energy, and influence behind someone else's goals. It requires you to take on some risk yourself and do it in the hopes of getting someone a better outcome in their career.

Think of the manager who didn't just tell you which opportunities you needed in your portfolio to be promotion-ready but *actively helped you find those opportunities*.

Think of the hiring manager who didn't just agree to your salary negotiation but *proactively reminded you that you can negotiate when making the offer*.

Think of the department leader who didn't just make an announcement saying they care about your mental health but *intentionally reached out to offer time off and resources when they saw you struggle*.

Think of the mentor who didn't just listen to your stories and observations but also *probed deeper and asked you what you wanted from your career and how they could help*.

All these examples and more are people you would want on your side. You would thank these people publicly if you became a big celebrity or won a Nobel prize. People don't forget kindness and compassion, and appreciate it even more when it comes unprompted and without strings attached. It is a privilege in your career if you get to be that ray of light in someone else's career!

As a Peer

You don't have to have more power and equity than someone to help them. You can do a lot as a colleague, a trusted friend, or even their junior. The main thing is to have the intention, back it up with real action, and provide what is needed. For self-advocacy, offering that support becomes even more essential because it is a skill that benefits from social feedback and suggestions.

Many people need reassurance and support when advocating for themselves in a tough situation. They may be facing challenges at work that they must address head-on, unsure how to ask for a raise or a promotion, or disengaging from a toxic situation. These situations can be stressful and isolating. People differ in tactics; no rule book dictates how to manage the situation. Depending on the people involved, even the best-intentioned advice can have unintended consequences! Offering unconditional support and encouragement can be incredibly meaningful to people, even if you cannot directly endorse or sponsor their efforts.

My LinkedIn feed is full of people asking for help and expressing gratitude when individuals provide genuine service. It's been a tough job market in 2022 and 2023 for many folks working in technology, and the support people receive while trying to advocate for themselves in the job search rarely goes unnoticed or unappreciated. There are stories of people thanking folks who provided them with unprompted referrals. People who helped remind someone of what they were worth, so they didn't accept a lowball offer. People who stood up and called out their company's hiring practices that made it unfair for specific candidates, without which someone may have had an even smaller chance of landing a job. It is terrific when people show up and advocate for someone else or help them improve that skill, whether they are friends or strangers.

Helping Others Helps You

Making space to support others on their journeys is a healthy habit that pays you dividends. People appreciate anyone who makes genuine attempts to assist them. Great relationships rely on people showing up for you during high-pressure moments. These relationships can last your whole career! They will offer you support if and when you need it.

When asked, you can listen, offer advice and suggestions, or amplify their wins. Creating a safe space is good for them; you also learn from them. Hearing how they view the challenges they are facing can add perspective to your own challenges as well. Understanding the methods they are trying can give you ideas as well. Sometimes, it is easier to provide a suggestion to someone else rather than come up with it when you're struggling and stressed about an issue. You build your muscle when you practice with someone else.

Supporting someone else's self-advocacy journey is something you volunteer for. It is rarely an expectation, but it can be rewarding nevertheless! You should do it simply because it is a nice thing, but know that it benefits you in the process.

It's an Easy Win!

Knowing what someone else needs on their self-advocacy journey can be tricky because sometimes they may be unable to articulate where you can help. People who struggle with self-advocacy may be reluctant to ask friends and coworkers for help.

If you want to be proactive and care about someone else's career, here are a few prompts you can use to gauge where you could add the most value for them:

- Do I understand their strengths, and what are the best things to amplify?
- What forums do I have access to where highlighting their achievements will be meaningful?
- Who can I connect them to, or who can I encourage to sponsor them, which helps their career?
- What resources can I provide that align with their desire to grow?
- What challenges can I help them with by listening or problem-solving if asked?
- How can I provide timely encouragement and moral support to help them with their goals?
- How can I remind them of their valuable skills if they have lowered confidence or a diminished sense of self-worth?

- What examples can I share of mine or my observed self-advocacy that can inspire them?

There are many ways you can help someone else advocate for themselves. There is no perfect way to do it, but it is good to try.

Chapter 7
Self-Advocacy in the Real World: Navigating a Job Promotion

Job promotions are one of the ways employers can reward and retain great employees. When an employer promotes an employee, it signals that their work is valued and that the company is willing to renegotiate the employment contract. One that is worth more and has a higher title, more pay, greater responsibilities, or all of those combined.

It can also be significant to an employee to receive a promotion beyond the title, pay, and increased influence. Receiving recognition and acknowledgment is essential to most people. Nobody wants to feel invisible or have their efforts taken for granted. People want to know that their work matters and is worthy of reward.

Some people are lucky to work for companies that reward excellent work in a timely and proactive manner. Such recognition could be due to a robust process in the entire company or an incredible work sponsor - usually a manager or another colleague with seniority. A promotion generally follows a firm intention on the company's or work sponsor's part to actively show you the path that leads to career progression and help you along the way. If you are lucky enough to be in such a situation, consider yourself part of a small crowd blessed with exceptional management.

Unfortunately, most people will be in situations where they have to be proactive about their career progression. Even with a great sponsor, it is still a fantastic idea to create the future you desire. After all, you are answerable to yourself and know yourself and what you want. You are the CEO of your career.

If you feel you've done reward-worthy work but haven't yet received the rewards for it, don't be disheartened. If you have plenty of proof that you deserve a promotion, your lack of getting it says more about your company/manager than it does about you. A lack of advancement does not define your worth. And not everyone who receives a promotion has earned it—some land new opportunities through luck, timing, or ass-kissing.

However, you can be your best advocate and make the case to get what you want and deserve. Going through the process can also help clarify the hurdle you're facing. Is it a case of negligent oversight, inadequate budgets, or malicious intent?

Are You Ready for a Promotion?

If you're working hard, getting results, and increasing value for the company, you should be actively thinking about your promotion readiness. Build the muscle where you evaluate your promotion-readiness rather than waiting for someone else to tell you when it's time—building the skills where you care more about your own opinion than someone else's is an act of self-advocacy.

The promotion process in every company can be very different. However, some patterns still tend to repeat, at least across most tech companies. Understanding and using these patterns to get what you have rightfully earned can be a game changer.

Most companies keep the process vague. That is perhaps intentional in many companies that don't have a leveling guide. If everyone had a playbook, there would be more accountability on the company's part to reward employees consistently. Promotion processes remain opaque for the same reason companies avoid salary transparency. Typically, neither the process nor the result is equitable (even if unintentional), and businesses don't want to spend all their time justifying personnel decisions.

The vague process makes it harder to determine if you're ready but learn to trust your instincts. You know yourself, your work, and when it's time for the next step. You can also see who else is getting promoted and what increased skills they are demonstrating. Calibrating against those is also a great way to form your opinion on promotion readiness. If you're in doubt, go for it anyway! You'll still always learn more than you did before you tried. You'll hear a yes or a no. If the answer is no, ask for the rationale behind the decision. The "why" will help you formulate your next steps.

Creating an Effective Promotion Pitch

Before we dive into the tactical process of seeking a promotion, a reminder:

Treat yourself with compassion.

You've earned the right to go after what you want and be rewarded for your achievements.

You are capable of accepting challenges to enhance your career.

It's good to start with these reminders because seeking a promotion can feel overwhelming, especially if you haven't had to ask for one actively. In the perfect world, leaders we work with would proactively recognize talent and reward merit. Unfortunately, we don't live in an ideal world.

Promotions are hard work, even when they are not contentious. Landing the outcome you want requires time, energy, and a willingness to understand and play the game. I know a little something about promotion processes, through my own experience and from those I have mentored. Over my sixteen-year career, I have received numerous promotions. On three separate occasions, I advanced within a few months of joining a new company. I have also promoted many people who chose to work for me. In my last organization, five of my six direct reports were promoted at least once during the two years we worked together (the sixth was very senior already).

Promotions are not always easy and require upfront work to make a clear case, even when your manager supports you. Either way, review the steps on the following pages to get a sense of things that would be useful to think about as you (or you, along with your manager) make the case. Then we'll dive into the details. You can download a helpful worksheet at www.shailvi.com/self-advocacy-resources.html.

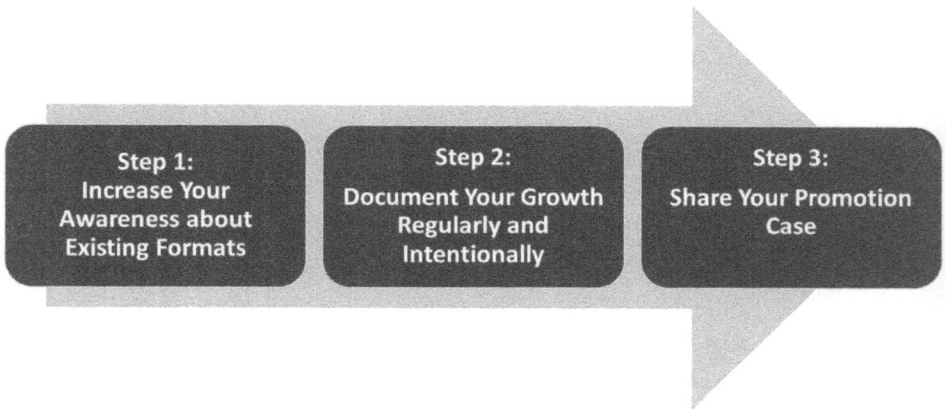

Step 1: Increase Your Awareness about Existing Formats	Step 2: Document Your Growth Regularly and Intentionally	Step 3: Share Your Promotion Case

Step 1: Increase Your Awareness about Existing Formats

Before you start compiling your case for a promotion, it is helpful to understand the promotion-readiness-related formats that already exist in your company, department, or team. Some companies are great at sharing this information proactively with all employees, whereas in other settings, you may have to ask for this information.

It is entirely valid to ask for help in finding these formats! You can have these conversations with your direct manager or HR business partner (or anyone in HR if your team doesn't have an assigned partner). If your company is cagey about sharing this information, that tells you something about the company and the level of transparency they want to offer regarding promotions. In those cases, the promotions are based on feelings or politics rather than being grounded in demonstrated, tangible merit. That is a problem since feelings are hard to quantify objectively. In such cases, you have options. You can dig in and get a sense of what is valued, push to have a more disciplined process, or decide whether going for a promotion in your current company is feasible. You can even choose to pursue all three options!

Another likely reason for the promotion format's opaqueness is favoritism. Unfortunately, many companies (or specific teams within a company) have a culture where flattery of people in positions of power will get you everywhere. Some leaders like to surround themselves with people who will say yes to everything they want, and those leaders are interested in something other than the growth of their team members. It is up to you to decide what you want to do with that information.

The knowledge of existing formats helps you learn what you need to focus on concerning your promotion case and teaches you valuable things about how managers in your company make decisions. This understanding enables you to set your expectations about what is realistic and the known boundaries.

Framework

See if there is an existing leveling guide available. Such manuals should have job titles outlined and clear expectations for each level. They could include skills (both technical and non-technical), the scope of projects, and the expectations for impact.

The guides can vary in different companies. Company-level guidelines may be vague, with more details provided for each function. For example, the Engineering and Product departments can have separate leveling guides aligned with the general company guidelines. It is useful when there is a guide based on the function since the examples are easier to comprehend. Some companies only have department or team-wide guides and nothing central to the company.

The level of detail included in the guidelines can vary quite a bit. Depending on your function, Google can be your friend since many companies have made their internal leveling guides public and easily searchable. Some companies even include specific details of the skills and provide guidelines about how someone must demonstrate competencies from the examples listed. These external level guides can be a great starting point, primarily if your company doesn't provide one already but is open to it!

It is good to view leveling guides and then reconcile them with who gets rewarded. That helps you see more real-world successes of people on your team whose work you know well and translate that into the promotion-readiness framework. An example leveling guide is available for download at www.shailvi.com/self-advocacy-resources.html.

If the guidelines are not available or helpful, ask for better material. Managers owe their teams better guidance on the path to career progression. That is their job. You are within your rights to ask what is required to reach the next level.

As a bonus, you can also offer to draft this up yourself if your manager is busy and won't prioritize this on your preferred timeline. You can find reasonable examples from friends and ex-colleagues in other companies to draft what it should look like and give management something to react to. Another source is your company's job description. If your company posted a job for the next level above you, that's a valuable guide to learning about expectations and skills sought out for that level!

With the knowledge of existing frameworks, you will better understand what information is most valuable to include in your promotion case so that it aligns with people's expectations.

People

There are two critical pieces to the people aspect of any existing promotion format:

1. Whose feedback is included?
2. Who needs to sign off?

Knowing these two pieces can help you align accordingly and determine who needs to be an audience when you self-advocate and amplify your work.

Many companies require all promotion cases to include subjective feedback. That feedback can be from your manager, peers, people who report to you, or those you lead. This feedback is essential for companies to make the promotion process less subjective. Calibrating multiple people's feelings adds more nuance to evaluating someone's performance. Understanding whose feedback will be included can help you stay anchored on the critical relationships you need to build and land.

Dig into as many details on the feedback portion as you can find out:

- How many people will the decision-makers ask?
- Will they ask specific people?
- Does someone's feedback have more weight?
- What questions will they ask?
- How far back will they go to identify the collaborators who can provide feedback?

Besides the feedback piece, the other key question is knowing who will eventually sign off. These can be multiple people, though your manager and HR are good starting points. It is rare for a promotion case to be approved if the direct manager doesn't endorse it. This is why many people move teams or companies entirely if they have landed a manager who doesn't support their growth. Similarly, getting past an HR non-endorsement can also be tricky. If HR has received reports of behavioral concerns or has other challenges about your promotion, it can be hard to bypass that. It is in your best interest to tackle any issues head-on if you feel they would be blockers to your promotion case from a sign-off perspective. Sometimes other people, such as department heads, key stakeholders, or a team lead need to provide approval. Knowing whose opinion counts is vital.

For all people-related pieces, be objective about what feedback people you work with have about you and how you can proactively shift those to more positive sentiments. If you are unsure how your colleagues feel about you, ask! People respond well to others who want to grow, and most people will try to give an honest answer to something as simple as "What advice would you have for me to improve and grow my skills?"

Timing

Even if your company has no set promotion guidelines, processes, or formats (I am silently judging these companies), they will still provide guidance about timing. The easiest way to articulate this is through two improbable scenarios: it is unlikely someone will be promoted within ten days of being hired, and it is unlikely someone will get promoted within ten days of their last promotion.

Most companies try to have set promotion cycles. Usually, these align with a performance review cadence. Companies that do a formal performance review decide in advance when and how often they will evaluate the performance of all employees. Using that as a prompt to determine who performs at the next level and is ready for promotion is common.

Companies can decide to only consider promotions at a half-yearly or yearly cadence or something else entirely. Employees who are unaware of these timing-related guidelines can get frustrated; they may have to wait months before their company can reach a decision. Taking steps to understand the cadence also benefits your mental peace.

Often the promotion timing can span multiple cycles. It would be unusual for many companies that review performance regularly to suddenly have an employee promoted if they hadn't been flagged as "almost ready" in the previous cycle. Many such company, departmental, or team nuances about timing could be at play.

Some companies don't have a specific cadence and consider promotions at any time, but they will still require the review of relevant and timely paperwork. Know how far ahead you need to submit documentation before a promotion decision can be made. It could be that the due diligence takes time or that management wants a cooling-off period between consensus and formal approval. Since promotions also tend to come with a salary bump, it is natural that companies will not want to make this decision overnight.

Step 2: Document Your Growth Regularly and Intentionally

Anything related to your promotion case, which evolves, requires regular and intentional documentation. Even if you just got a promotion yesterday, start building the documentation for your next promotion. Consistently anchor at showing progression towards the next level.

Doing this also helps you stay focused on your skills and growth beyond just the promotion moment in your current role. Sometimes, you may realize your opportunities are stale, and you must find other ways to stretch yourself.

Start with the eight pieces below, as they can form the basis of promotion documentation:

Scope of Role

These are the basics of your role and its unique value to the business.

- What business problems does your role solve?
- What business problems can your role solve in the future?
- What negative impact does the business face if your position doesn't exist?

These factors align to the role and not specifically about you. Your position exists to solve a specific problem for the business. Unless your responsibilities are specific to a company niche, the role also likely exists in other companies. Starting with that shared understanding is an excellent way to align on the fundamental piece: your job exists because it is essential for the company's success. Next, you can focus on why you are uniquely successful.

Experience

Highlighting your experience that makes you a perfect fit for the role is vital in helping people understand your value.

- What's your background (e.g., education, prior jobs.) related to the role?
- What makes you uniquely qualified to add value?
- What niche experiences do you have that are hard to replicate?

People should have a clear understanding of your experience and credentials. Sometimes educational qualifications are helpful; sometimes, it is years of work experience or a mix of the two. More important than either of those pieces might be that you have specific domain knowledge (either due to your time in the current company or working in the same industry) that is valuable to the company's success.

Ensuring people understand the niche experiences that directly help the company and are not easily replaceable with another candidate highlights your unique value.

Track Record

It isn't enough to be qualified for your role. You must show the results.

- What tangible wins have you had in technical projects (using core skills related to your function)?
- What specific results did you achieve in your work?
- What is the impact of your work on the company's bottom line?
- What examples show how you demonstrated leadership and company values?

People care about results, and they want to see clear examples of that. They want to see you doing things that matter and achieving results. Otherwise, you cannot advance! Making decisions and executing tasks that drive revenue or reduce costs is more often perceived as valuable. Doing more work where you are successful matters, so take the time to pick the best projects!

It is important to phrase your track records in line with the expectations of your role and your target level. If you feel your track record doesn't quite align with expectations at more senior levels, ask for help finding opportunities to demonstrate those higher performance levels.

Be specific and cite numbers and objective data when articulating your track record. Even if your role is providing services to another team, you can ask that partner team for tangible data to show your work's impact. It is good to focus on the effects of your work and not just that you were assigned a task and got it done. Corporate leaders value critical thinking. Showing that you are focused on the impact—and not just checking off your to-do list—goes a long way in building your credibility.

The more senior your role, the more you will need to demonstrate both technical success and leadership skills. These dual criteria are not just for those who are in explicit people leadership roles. Individual contributors must demonstrate these skills too. It is essential that senior talent show that they can guide others, create followership, and help align people with a common goal.

Most companies also are open about their company values and expect employees to care about them. Showing that direct connection between how you work and espouse those values can be powerful. Whether your company cares about flawless execution, kindness to colleagues, or giving back to the community, include specific examples.

Feedback

The positive feedback you have received for your performance can be critical to a successful promotion case.

- What kudos have you received in the past from peers?
- What praise has come your way from superiors?
- Are there people who like collaborating with you whom you could ask for a specific quote?
- Is there critical feedback your manager provided before, which you have since addressed?

In nearly every job, one of the first things I do is create a kudos folder. It is hard to track when you receive praise, so when someone does so in an email or a comment on a project or chat thread, I make a note of it and add it to my kudos folder. If someone praises me verbally, I note it down. If I have a good relationship with them, I also ask if they would be open to directly sharing that feedback with my boss.

Creating this body of organic feedback (usually unprompted and different from requests for input as part of performance reviews) can be especially useful for a promo case. It shows that there are colleagues who are genuinely appreciative of your work and feel you add value. Of course, many colleagues are not forthcoming with unprompted praise, and it is perfectly acceptable to prompt them when you know you have provided value. This process also helps you find the right words to describe the impact of your work.

If you previously received guidance on improving, also include your progress on that. Some people could be shy to include negative comments they got in the past - but if you have addressed those pieces, it is great to include that. It shows a willingness to learn and proves you have a growth mindset.

Sponsors

A robust promotion case includes endorsements from influential sponsors.

- Who are relevant leaders who support your promotion?
- Who are peers whose opinion is valuable and who support your promotion?
- If you have potential detractors, whose endorsement can offset that?
- Which stakeholders with whom you regularly work can attest to your being ready for a promotion?

The absence of proactive sponsors for a promotion case isn't always a deal-breaker, but their presence dramatically increases the odds of getting your desired outcomes. Organizations that have a formal promotion process sometimes ask for a list of sponsors. In those situations, requests like this will come in, thus making it a little easier to ask a potential sponsor for support.

If you do not belong to such an organization, you can ask potential sponsors directly. For example, you might say, "I am looking to grow in my career and will be ready for a promotion soon. Would you have any feedback for me to grow my skills, or would you be comfortable endorsing my promotion case? I respect your opinion a lot!" This script will generally work in environments where open feedback is normalized. Of course, if someone doesn't want to support your promotion and doesn't know how to say so to your face, that might be awkward. You can circumvent that awkwardness by either going after people with whom you feel a high degree of confidence or sending an optional anonymous survey to a select group of potential allies.

Learn whose opinion counts. You may be under the illusion that your promotion is a given since all your teammates rave about your work. However, if it's primarily the stakeholder opinion that matters, and they have many complaints, you're not in a good spot. It doesn't matter whether you think the stakeholders' views shouldn't matter. What matters is what is expected. Being strategic about whom to keep happy and engaged with your work is an important skill to build. Sometimes you could have difficult sponsors whose opinion of you is hard to change, but you can still circumvent that situation by going after someone else whose opinion matters more.

Performance Reviews

Your manager's formal feedback in regular career conversations is integral to the promotion case.

- What were the successes highlighted in your last few performance reviews?
- What were areas of growth highlighted, and how have you made progress?
- What was the rating given for your overall performance?

Companies with a formal performance review process add more transparency to the promotion process. If you are asked to recap your performance at a regular cadence, you are already in the habit of amplifying your wins to your boss. It is also going into consolidated documentation. If your manager is asked to recap your performance, then they either agree with your assessment of yourself, or provide feedback on their perspective with tangible next steps.

If your performance reviews have been positive, and you have been getting good ratings, a promotion case becomes easier. Every company may have its own quirks about how they look at these pieces with regard to a promotion (e.g., some companies require a few cycles of an "exceeds expectations" rating to even consider you for a promotion). As always, the aggregation of what you think makes sense and getting feedback on how it adds to your promotion case is still a very useful exercise, and it increases your knowledge about what it takes to get promoted in your organization.

You shouldn't be afraid of receiving feedback about what you can improve on during performance reviews. Many times, it can be a good thing! It often means that your manager actually cares about your growth and is giving you a better blueprint on how to succeed. Once you have acknowledged an area for improvement exists, you can be intentional about addressing it and seeking more ideas if you're struggling to improve that area. If you keep learning and growing by addressing your areas for improvement, you get that much closer to a promotion.

Time in Role

Shining a light on how long you have been in your current role and level can help with your promotion case.

- How long have you been in your current role?
- When were you last promoted?

Time spent in a role is not a fixed expectation. If you ask a company executive how long an Engineer should expect to work before being promoted to Senior Engineer, you might get a range as an answer or no answer at all. The path to a promotion depends on the individual. However, it is a helpful data point, especially compared to others in the same role.

If other people in similar roles received promotions after an average of two years, and you've been in the position for three years, management should be able to articulate a reason behind that. If you lack the necessary skills, your manager should be proactive in helping you grow in those areas and should ideally have provided you with regular feedback, including performance reviews.

If the company has changed its stance and requires management to slow down promotion rates, you should be aware of that increased bar or standards they have set. It could purely be a budget issue if the company doesn't have the money to pay for salary increases that usually come with a promotion. Your company may also have some unstated rules that require people to be in a role for a specified amount of time before being eligible for promotion. Information is your friend, and it always helps to have more of it.

Peers

Other people in the role at the level you're going after can help add perspective to your promotion case.

- Who are your peers in your target role/level?
- What are the similarities in your experiences and impact?
- What are some key differences in your qualifications?

Promotions are by nature comparative, the need for which is easier to comprehend when highlighting similarities in work output. Unfortunately, people who don't sufficiently publicize their work are slower to get promotions, even if they get great results. It is helpful to compare your impact with that of someone with a higher rank. Ideally, it should be framed as a business-savvy decision to give you the same level of influence through the promotion and title change as someone with similar quality results. The company wins when talented people are in positions of success!

Sometimes management might get defensive when you share a comparison and give reasons why the other person deserved the promotion and you do not. It is in your best interest to preempt that defensiveness by stating you are trying your best to understand what you need to do to get ready for promotion through real and relatable examples of your colleagues.

Some companies have promotion quotas. For example, only 10 percent of employees can get promoted during a single promotion cycle. In these cases, promotions are relative. Anybody performing at the next level is essentially being stack ranked, and then a line is drawn with the number of job promotions a company is willing to give out. This approach is the reality in some companies, and the tolerance for flexibility varies. Especially for senior positions, there can be situations where there can't be more than a certain number of people at a particular level. For example, a company may decide there can't be more than one Vice President of Data at a time.

Overall, creating this documentation should give you the perspective to go after a promotion armed with knowledge and relevant data points. Even if the information changes rarely, develop a habit of keeping your documentation up-to-date!

Step 3: Share Your Promotion Case

The best promotion cases are the ones you actively pursue. It doesn't matter if you feel 100 percent confident about the outcome or not confident at all. If you've done the work, then shoot your shot. Often, just going through the process adds a ton of clarity to your mind. It also helps the person you are making the promotion case to get clarity on your goals and how serious you are about them.

When I was hosting the Grace Hopper Conference mentoring circle for Self-Advocacy in 2019, I met a woman who shared her story of seeking a promotion. She said it took her three tries to get the outcome she sought. The first time she simply asked her manager if she could get promoted. Her manager was surprised by the request and gave her some broad but firm reasons why she wasn't ready for a promotion yet. The second time, she documented improvements in many of the gaps her manager had highlighted and presented a more coherent case. Her manager saw that she took the process seriously and gave her more detailed feedback. By her final attempt, she had a much deeper understanding of what her manager cared about and what she could do to showcase her performance at the next level. Her manager also, by then, knew what she was aiming for and was more proactive about helping her. Her final attempt was a success, and she felt better prepared for any future promotions she planned to go after.

Seeking a promotion can feel overwhelming, and there is no formula for guaranteed success. All you can do is make your best attempt and learn something valuable from the process, regardless of the outcome. By taking the first step to formalize seeking a promotion, you already show your ability to problem-solve and be intentional.

There are three steps in making your promotion case:

1. Consolidated documentation
2. Getting help
3. Presenting your case

Consolidate Your Documentation

Review all the information you compiled in Step 2. Decide what information you want to share directly with someone who is a decision-maker for your promotion. Some information might be helpful for you to keep track of, while other information is a critical component of convincing someone else to act on your promotion proposal.

Consolidate all the pieces you feel are relevant into a consumable format. Stay anchored on the story you want to tell and your desired outcome. What do you want your audience to feel? What do you want them to see? What do you want them to do? Creating a compelling story for why you have earned your promotion and keeping the context of who will review that story front and center can help you stay on the message. Play around with proven storytelling formats (for example, a linear narration that shows your progress or a case study on how you have added value) and pick the one that resonates with your needs and would be effective for your specific audience.

The last time I made a successful case for my promotion, I divided the documentation into the different forums I would discuss with my manager. I mapped out the default self-review process and realized my manager would read it asynchronously. I noted which bullet points I would address in our next one-on-one meeting. I also considered potential things he might say and how I'd respond. And finally, I put together a formal document that outlined my request for a promotion. I shared this document with my manager as a pre-read before our one-on-one conversation, and it included links to my latest self-performance review. Feeling prepared on all three fronts took work, but it helped me feel more confident about the outcome! In your case, think about the documentation and the formats that make sense for you in your situation.

Remember to keep things organized and follow a logical flow. You may not execute flawlessly in the first go, but you can iterate as often as needed!

Get Help

Getting help from your network as you compile your promotion case can be a practical strategy. Count on your trusted friends, colleagues, mentors, coaches, or anyone who can provide valuable feedback. They can help you understand the tone or your pitch, advise on the right words and phrases, or even provide a practice audience.

A former colleague of mine was great at doing the work but could have done better at talking about it. He was reluctant to draw attention to his work and the impact he had. He was very well-liked and respected on the team and was often the one whom people sought help from when they encountered challenges. That didn't prevent him from being passed over for promotion multiple times because leadership didn't feel he was doing promotion-worthy work.

When he shared his frustration with me and another colleague, we both offered to help. We knew our team would be less successful if he wasn't around, and we were eager to ensure our leaders understood the value he added. As we pointed out all that he had achieved, he realized he had been highlighting his reputation and not his results, even though his results were the driving force behind that reputation! Making sure he clearly articulated that to our leadership became his next goal. Trusted well-wishers can often help provide critical feedback and help you see the path that could yield better results.

Having people you trust, who care about you and your career, review your promotion case can be a huge morale boost. Sometimes, they add things you forgot about your accomplishments and why you earned your promotion.

Present Your Case

After you have compiled your promotion case and got feedback from friends, present it! Do it with confidence and conviction. The decision-makers for your promotion case need to understand your excellent work.

The default person to present your promotion case to is your manager. However, there can be many situations where you have tried and failed to get their time, or they have dismissed it outright without even hearing you out. In those cases, determine the next-best audience with the right influence and power to support your promotion case. It may be your department head or a member of human resources. Either way, it is your career and life, so take this to the logical conclusion if the first try doesn't work out.

You may not receive the desired reaction to your promotion case. Life would be easy if we all got what we wanted the first time we tried! In the scenario where you have yet to convince someone that you are ready for a promotion, the next best thing that can happen is that they understand it matters to you and commit to helping you get where you want to be. The worst thing that can happen is they find you accusatory, entitled, or out of touch with reality. The latter is the reaction you want to avoid. Framing the promotion conversation as a learning opportunity, where you can better understand what is possible and come to a reasonable level of alignment, is an excellent way to prevent that adverse reaction.

Seeking a promotion can be an emotional experience for you as someone seeking it. The person to whom you present your case may feel defensive or conflicted. They may worry that you view them as not doing enough for your career. They could worry you'll be unhappy if you don't get what you want and leave. They could fear five other team members will expect a promotion if they grant you one. There will always be a mixture of rational and irrational thoughts on the receiver's part, and you can't possibly preempt them all. You will have the best chance of success if you come prepared, know your boundaries, and customize your communication to the specific person and what you know about them.

In all cases, practice your authentic voice in which you highlight your achievements and your needs. You are not asking for a favor with a promotion case. Businesses should reward people who add value. Talk about yourself the way your best friend would talk about you. They would never underplay your achievements or ask you to settle.

Seeking a promotion requires courage and tenacity. If you step onto this path, you deserve much applause just for attempting it. It can be an emotional but gratifying process and well worth the investments you make in your career!

Chapter 8
Self-Advocacy in the Real World: Negotiating Compensation

Why does an employer give you a job offer that includes a salary? Because the business needs your skills to succeed, and the company benefits from your work.

Start with that essential reminder. Do not think of compensation as a favor your company is doing for you. You choose to spend hours in your day working. Some people do it for the pure joy of work and would happily work for free. But it is understandable if you're not one of them. Your choice to spend your time working for a particular employer deserves to be compensated appropriately based on the value you add. Companies are getting something tangible out of it. If nobody works for a company, their business doesn't exist. Even in the case of a mostly automated process, a human has to set up and maintain the robots and automation.

A salary is a transaction between two consenting parties, labor for money. If you remove the emotion, it is just a number that should meet your needs and makes business sense to the company. Figuring out the correct number for yourself and who will give you that number or more is a great skill to develop!

Most salary numbers result from negotiations. Your self-advocacy and savviness in that situation can make a big dent in something that impacts your daily life from that point on until the next salary negotiation. It is essential to give that negotiation its due care and focus.

Steps to a satisfying negotiation:

1. Self-awareness about your needs
2. Research on market realities
3. Clear articulation about the value you provide

Self-Awareness: Understanding Your Needs

The first step to any successful salary negotiation is to know what you want. Not what your friend wants, not what will give your mother bragging rights, or what your college roommate will find impressive. Know what *you* want.

Everyone individually has aspirations and things that bring them joy. Narrowing down the specifics of what you care about can help you negotiate for the right pieces. Nobody should work for less than their worth or less than what's fair. But beyond a range, more money doesn't equal more satisfaction, and that's important to remember during a negotiation. Ultimately, during a negotiation, you want to advocate for your whole self, not just your financial self.

Minimum Salary Threshold

Coming up with a base minimum number is the easy part. You have a lifestyle, bills to pay, savings to create for future safety and a psychological threshold that makes you comfortable. A salary should account for that, and this sets your absolute minimum number. If this isn't your first job, then you also have a benchmark of your last salary and how well it did or didn't meet your monetary needs. This knowledge can help you figure out what the new wage needs to be.

If a salary doesn't meet your minimum threshold, you must either look for additional income sources or scale back your lifestyle. It may even involve adapting your risk tolerance and willingness to rely on contingency plans. Only you know how realistic any of those options are! Understanding these pieces sets the intention behind the importance of meeting that minimum number below which you would not accept an offer and keep looking.

A minimum salary is by no means what you should accept. It just sets a benchmark below which you shouldn't even interview. It is better to spend time pursuing opportunities that meet our needs.

Career Values

Contrary to traditional wisdom, money isn't the only thing we get out of a job. We all have individual desires, and even those can change over time. Human beings are complex, and our aspirations are nuanced. We cannot be reduced to simple equations.

Figuring out everything you want from a job is vital so you can use salary negotiation as leverage. As I have said, more money beyond a basic threshold doesn't always lead to more happiness. Some people care about power and authority and would happily trade a percentage of their salary if it meant more of that. Others may have a work-life balance as a non-negotiable, and they would need a *lot* more money even to consider adjusting that balance. The work you do is valuable as well. We choose a particular profession for a reason. There may be no amount of money that would make you give up a satisfying role or a great work environment for good reasons.

A few years ago, my coach introduced me to the concept of career values, and it has been one of the most powerful tools for my job-related decision-making since then.[7] The prompt is simple: "What do I want from work?" The idea is to develop a stack-ranked list of three to five values you prioritize above all else you need to satisfy. What do you want to maximize? Where do you need to meet a minimum threshold? Use the list below to begin brainstorming:

- Authenticity
- Autonomy
- Camaraderie
- Creativity
- Fun
- Intellectual growth
- Power

---

[7] Indeed Editorial Team. "Career Values: How to Identify Yours and Cultivate Success as ... - Indeed." *Indeed.Com*, www.indeed.com/career-advice/career-development/career-values. Accessed 11 Aug. 2023.

- Stability
- Work-life balance

Create your stack-ranked list and consider what you can ask for during an offer negotiation. What deal-breakers would prevent you from even applying for a job? What are you trying to maximize? What are you willing to trade for a lower salary (but still above your minimum threshold)? Knowing what you truly care about can go a long way in a successful negotiation!

Ideal Scenario

- ✓ Write down what makes you happy at work and what you want out of it.
- ✓ Look at it and visualize it.
- ✓ Add intention to make it a reality.

As you think about minimum salary thresholds and career values, don't forget to focus on the big-picture aspirations. Aspirations are good, and they help us go after them with more intention. You more effectively advocate for yourself when you know the ideal scenario you are going after.

Whatever aspects of an offer and a new role excite you, note them down. Normalize thinking about them when you look at job postings and talk to recruiters. Cut out the noise and eliminate job options that don't value what you value. If that makes your pool of acceptable jobs too small, revamp your scenarios to see where you are most flexible. But if you have plenty of options, and it is just a matter of landing the right one, hold firm!

Research Market Realities

Research and discover your market worth, including the industry averages and location. There are many nuances to an individual's market worth and the nuances that go into quantifying your experience and skills. Unfortunately, there is no exact science, just a lot of information you can use as benchmarks. Websites like Glassdoor, Paysa, and Levels.fyi are great places to start looking for these benchmarks.

Besides your market worth, there is also the nuance of what a company is willing and able to pay. A big company and a small startup will have very different paying capacities. They offer different benefits regarding learning, autonomy, and future upside. You can go after the right opportunities once you reconcile what they offer with your needs. Just keep in mind that a company defines its budget and standards, and it may only sometimes be able to meet offers from a competing company. Knowing what each company offers you personally can help you pitch for the right offer package.

It can also be constructive to ask real people you know who are willing to share their salaries to get a better sense of what to ask for. This advice is especially valuable for early-career professionals or those starting in a new industry. I've known many people who moved to tech from academia and were surprised they were getting 50% less than what was fair for their role because they never asked for more. In these cases, the companies are wrong for paying someone so much below the market rate just because they didn't ask for more. Still, the outcome could have been very different if the person had advocated for themselves by doing their research and asking for the correct number.

Asking people or looking at data points online can also have downsides. People are not always truthful on anonymous internet forums, and they may inflate or deflate their actual compensation. It is easier for large companies or common roles to triangulate the correct number because of the sheer volume of data points available. Calibration becomes much more challenging for niche roles or small companies.

If you seek anecdotes from people you know, they might not represent market realities. Small sample sizes often result in skewed data. People from marginalized groups tend to have lower salaries. When I was graduating from college, the reverse was true for me. As a woman of color in technology, I was part of a significantly underrepresented group. But all my anecdotal data points of what salaries should look like were from men since I didn't have many female fellow students. My salary thus got anchored higher than what I had started with in my head.

Never undersell yourself.

You are being fair to yourself and to the company, which won't have to deal with an employee who is later resentful for being underpaid.

It helps to set realistic expectations for yourself based on market realities. Knowing what's possible and what's realistic can help you go after the right opportunities confidently. It also lets you prioritize your time since finding and applying for jobs is laborious and time-consuming. You may make better decisions on what you do with your time if you know the possible outcome.

Clearly Articulate the Value You Provide

When you find an opportunity you love, and it loves you back, respect the potential new relationship and try to come to a fair deal. Ironing out specifics early, setting expectations, and being willing to listen (not just be heard) are great ways to start.

Some companies offer signing bonuses, stock, or relocation packages. The more you know about the specific company and what it provides, the better prepared you'll be to get a good deal. All companies expect you to negotiate. You won't offend anyone if you are polite and provide well-structured thoughts on why you are asking for this or that.

Remind Yourself of Your Own Needs and Preferences

Before you even receive an offer, and whenever you are close to the final stages of a job interview process, remind yourself of your needs and preferences. Review your monetary conditions, career values, and what perks and benefits are meaningful. If you have open questions about the role itself or what the opportunity would mean for your growth, it is helpful to have those consolidated as well.

It is good to organize these pieces before you receive the offer so that you are prepared and can bring up things appropriately.

Understand the Offer and Identify Next Steps

Once you receive an offer, you should always thank the company for making the offer. Thank them for their time and thoughtfulness.

You can then ask for more details about the offer and get any clarifying information sorted out. If you care about benefits and might use those to negotiate, ask for more information on those as well. Expect that they don't have every piece available for you immediately and will send some details via email later.

It is typical and expected to request some time to think about and reflect on the offer. You can reiterate that you are excited about the company/role/offer but ask for a fixed amount of time to consider it more. Mention that there are a few areas where you'd like to negotiate. You don't have to mention specifics at this time. Just say you need to process the information so you can respond thoughtfully. Consider using this opportunity to mention competing offers. You don't have to give all the details but don't bluff either, as that can spectacularly backfire. If you're planning to negotiate (which you should!), ideally, don't wait more than one business day to respond with a counteroffer.

131

A negotiation should honor the time of both parties, and it's helpful to outline the plan early and clearly. Let whoever is making the offer know what you intend to do between now and your stated timeline, and stick to the timetable.

Define the Monetary Components

Pick the higher number between your minimum salary threshold and your researched market reality! Pick the higher number and then add 20 percent. That should be your starting point for any negotiation.

Think about all the monetary aspects such as bonus pay, equity grants, 401(k) matching, stipends, and perks that save you the money you are already spending (e.g., childcare costs). While these may not be negotiable as they are standardized offerings (bonus and equity being the significant exceptions), they can change the equation considerably. Only add up the monetary aspects you can and will use. For example, a pet insurance stipend is meaningless if you don't have pets. Gather these financial details and see how that compares with your personal base number.

Many startups offer a lower base pay and try to make it up in terms of equity. The idea is that you are taking a hit on your cash compensation right now, on the potential of the equity being worth more. Only you can decide how much of a blow to base pay you can take. Equity can be a risky bet, especially for non-public companies. The current equity value reflects what the company's investors think it's worth. The future value is also unproven. Also, the equity is illiquid, and you can't freely exchange it for cash. Talk to a trusted financial advisor to understand your options and what risks you can take. In addition to that, do some research and do the math.

Define Negotiable Perks

As you think about the monetary aspects of the offer and how that compares with your expectations, note non-monetary perks. You can negotiate those once you are satisfied with the financial components.

Some perks are standardized and available to all employees. These include paid time off, food and beverage options, learning and development stipends, access to unique venues or services, and work-from-home opportunities. Based on what matters to you, you ask for tweaks or additional padding on these perks. If the default work-from-home expectation is two days a week, but you need three, ask for that upfront. If you have a specific reason to request a more significant learning and development stipend, and you can demonstrate the benefit to your employer, find a way to articulate that. Remember that the employer wants to meet your needs. It means you'll be happier at the job and more likely to put in your best work.

Some perks could be specific to just your role or level. You may be a senior executive, and you could be assigned an Executive Assistant who can help you run things more smoothly. Or you, as part of the engineering team, can take additional days off to attend specific conferences. The company may be able to compensate you for your volunteer hours toward a worthy cause. Understand what's negotiable and prioritize what is meaningful to you. A good employer will proactively share information about these options! Employers with little flexibility on the monetary elements can be surprisingly flexible on the non-monetary factors.

The crucial part is to be aware of any specifics of the offer and what you'd want out of it. The package may include many benefits and bonuses; only you can tell what's relevant.

Establish Your Boundaries

Establish your boundaries after determining your monetary and non-monetary preferences for the job offer. Define what is non-negotiable for you and what things you want to maximize. It is helpful to craft that before you decide how to communicate it to the potential employer to maximize your likelihood of getting what you want.

It is better to focus on the core pieces you need from the offer negotiation rather than go after ten different small parts. Think about the elements that would have the most significant positive impact. One of the ways you can do that is by stack-ranking your "wish list" of the improvements you want to see in the offer. Think about feasibility as well based on what you know about the employer and the market conditions, and revise that stack-ranked list.

Pitch

A good pitch template for negotiating a job offer includes the following key components:

- What you want
- How you frame the pitch
- Why you are making the pitch
- To whom you will pitch
- When will you pitch
- Where will you pitch

Draft a pitch outlining **what** you want. It should contain details of the various pieces on your wish list and any rigid boundaries you have (e.g., you cannot accept the offer unless your salary meets a certain threshold, or your title meets specific criteria). Be clear, precise, and reasonable in outlining your what.

How you frame the pitch matters. If your salary needs are a nice-to-have rather than a deal-breaker, don't say you will only accept the job offer at a higher salary. Instead, you can say, "I'd feel much better about accepting an offer that includes tuition reimbursement." You don't want an employer to call your bluff and rescind the offer or make an offer to their alternate candidate. So be clear about your boundaries and stick to them.

Add the **why** behind your request. Include external data highlighting market realities, your needs, and why the extra negotiation matters. It is helpful for employers to understand the context behind why you made the particular pitch and how you came up with the suggestions. If this should help you as a thoughtful and fair person in the negotiation, it dramatically increases your odds of getting what you want.

Be clear about to **whom** you are making the pitch. Usually, the person who made the offer is the recruiter or the hiring manager. It could be that the decision-maker is somebody else, so you can ask to connect with that person directly.

As highlighted earlier, you should have a clear timeline for **when** you will negotiate after receiving the initial offer. Stick to that timeline. Also, don't make the negotiation a ten-step process. You should ideally not have an endless back-and-forth. Once you request a modification, the company representative will return with a confirmation or a counteroffer. Think hard before making additional counteroffers from your side unless you really won't accept the offer without additional revisions.

Where you should make the pitch depends on the complexity. Negotiate live (in person or on the phone) whenever possible. Synchronous negotiations minimize miscommunication and allow you to clarify any areas of ambiguity. However, if your pitch is very complicated, it is better to share it in a written format before the live conversation so that the audience can absorb and process it better.

You will have to make many judgment calls in your final pitch. Take the time you need to develop an authentic approach that effectively advocates for your needs. Research, ask for feedback from well-wishers, and go after what you want. A well-constructed pitch is worth the time you need to get it right. Good luck! You've got this!

Chapter 9
Self-Advocacy in the Real World: Happiness

One of the biggest acts of self-advocacy is adding clarity and intention to your plan for joy. Without joy, we risk burnout, and our careers can be severely limited. Our work makes up a big part of our days, our months and years, and our life. If we spend most of our life unhappy, that is quite a waste!

Focusing on happiness requires us not just to pursue happiness but prioritize it. Happiness isn't something we get by doing something or buying something; it is an intentional choice we make by prioritizing it daily. Just like every other muscle we build for self-improvement, happiness is a muscle that requires regular exercise. This deliberate, sustained effort leads us to more satisfying lives and careers.

The four phases of prioritizing happiness:
1. Awareness
2. Acknowledgment
3. Acceptance
4. Action

Awareness

To prioritize happiness, we must first be aware of what truly brings us joy—awareness of ourselves, why something brings us joy, and what we want.

Adding clarity to our plan for joy takes work. External factors can often muddle our need for pleasure. Social media has opinions on what will bring us joy and bombards us with content and advertisements designed to make us want certain things. Our friends and family can have their take on what makes them happy. Consequently, they assume that will make us happy as well. Society, in general, has taken on "default" joy generators, and you're never far from those reminders.

Shutting down all the external noise and focusing on what truly matters to you is hard work, but it can be significant. A common theme came up during my mentoring sessions. Many people spent years chasing careers they didn't want. They stayed on an unfulfilling path until they sat down to sift through what they truly cared about.

The first questions we must ask ourselves are, "What is it in life that we hope to maximize? What are those few things that make us feel at ease and ready to accept joy?" To get better at prioritizing joy, we must understand it and add clarity.

Happiness at the Community Level

Happiness can mean many things to people, especially if you try to quantify it for large groups. A handy framework I learned of many years ago was from countries that measured happiness and reported it in aggregate. Bhutan is the pioneer in this area, as it was the first country to decide that it wouldn't just care about GDP (Gross Domestic Product) but instead it would measure, report and try to improve GNH (Gross National Happiness). [8]

For Bhutan, a tiny mountain kingdom in the Himalayas, it is essential that they try to maximize happiness for their citizens, in line with what they value as a country. For that, they came up with the GNH Index (first measured in 2008) that tried to quantify the happiness levels of individuals and consolidate the results across the country. Surveys record responses to questions about specific indicators. There are thirty-three indicators across nine broad domains, none directly measuring

---

[8] Sithey, Gyambo, et al. "Gross National Happiness and Health: Lessons from Bhutan." *Bulletin of the World Health Organization*, 1 Aug. 2015, www.ncbi.nlm.nih.gov/pmc/articles/PMC4581665/.

happiness. Instead, they are related to everyday experiences that *contribute* to happiness, such as:

- Health
- Time Use
- Social Relationships
- Growth Opportunities
- Living Standards

It is an exciting concept and fascinating how they execute it. For each of the indicators, they measure if it meets a "sufficient threshold." For example, "Is an individual getting at least eight hours of sleep every day?" or "Has an adult received at least six years of formal schooling?"

I visited Bhutan on an incredible trip many years ago and learned first-hand how their quest for happiness has affected public policy in many tangible ways. The citizens take pride in their culture and in caring for the environment. They have advocated for environmental goals (that they often exceed) that directly improve health, living standards, and cultural preservation, which positively impact social relationships.

As Bhutan created and adopted this process in their country, they also shared their knowledge with the rest of the world. By 2012, the United Nations had also committed to measuring and publishing the World Happiness Report.[9] The report is compiled every year across the world. Some domains are similar to Bhutan's index, although they have a broader framing. UN's report measures:

- Life expectancy
- Freedom of Choice
- Social Support
- Generosity
- Trust & Corruption
- GDP per capita

---

[9] Helliwell, John F., et al. "World Happiness Report 2023." *The World Happiness Report*, 20 Mar. 2023, worldhappiness.report/ed/2023/.

The UN's methodology is similar to, but different from, the Bhutanese measurement in some fundamental ways. Its criteria are quantifiable and less subjective. In addition to that, I love the addition of generosity as one of the domains, as studies back it as a contributor to happiness.

Happiness for the Individual

Both Bhutan and the UN report data in aggregate, but how do they help you figure out what you care about? If someone had asked me years ago if I was happy, my answer would have been a qualitative assessment of my feelings and probably anchored to my recency bias. Feelings are notoriously hard to measure and inconsistent to record. Recent events and future possibilities can heavily influence our level of happiness.

For this reason, a good framework prompts you to think about the indicators that are not directly about the feeling but, when optimized, can lead to that feeling. The framework can be more helpful than a simple yes or no question of "Are you happy?"

I put together this framework based partly on the two measurement philosophies above, the one from Bhutan and the one from the UN. Use the prompts below to start thinking about the components that matter to you. You can also download my "Happiness for the Individual" worksheet at www.shailvi.com/self-advocacy-resources.html.

- Do I prioritize my health?
    - o Physical health: Getting enough exercise, good sleep, and quality nutrition
    - o Mental health: Managing stress, anxiety, and emotional stability
- Do I use my time on things I care about?
    - o Relaxation: Getting enough time to unwind, take a vacation, go out in the sun
    - o Creativity: Spending time on hobbies, music, art
    - o Play: Doing activities that bring me joy, like sports and movies
- Do I have growth opportunities?

- o Work: The ability to do meaningful work that satisfies you and effectively utilizes your skills
- o Learn: The ability to grow your skills, learn new things, and get an education
- o Contribute: Freedom to shape your daily life through fair government, contribution to your community, and alignment with local policies
- Do I meet the thresholds for the living standards I care about?
  - o Money: For many, this is a means to an end and needs a certain threshold to be met based on the life you want
  - o Lifestyle: Your home, modes of transportation, and ability to buy certain material goods, are all part of the lifestyle you care about
  - o Discretionary spending: You may care about being able to travel or pursue specific interests that require money, time, or both
- Can I invest time in social relationships I care about?
  - o Family: The ability to spend enough time with family and take care of responsibilities
  - o Friends: Time to invest in friendships and to show up for people you care about
  - o Community: The ability to give back to society, build connections you care about, and create a sense of belonging with a community you value

Everyone has different priorities, and those priorities can also change over time. When we are younger, focusing on nutrition and mental health is less prominent; as we age, we may feel that free time is more important than money. In all situations, check in with yourself to understand what is essential for your happiness and well-being.

Acknowledgment

Being intentional about prioritizing happiness requires acknowledging and appreciating things going well. Prioritizing happiness is a journey, not a destination. The process involves expressing gratitude, reflecting on how things are going, and noting what changes you might want to make.

Thank the Universe

Show gratitude for all the little things that are going well, which bring you joy. Happiness isn't always in the big moments. Frequently, it is a series of small things that bring us joy. Some of these may happen because you intentionally sought ways to make those positive experiences happen. Sometimes, things go well, even unintentionally.

It can be challenging to see how exactly things are adding up for the absence of pain to be a reality. So many things are outside our control, and it is hard to fathom the number of things that had to go right before you got to experience something that made you happy. When you take a moment to reflect for a moment and express gratitude for that unexpected source of joy, it increases your happiness. First, you notice that moment, which increases the time you spend thinking about something joyful. Second, you focus on the source of joy. Even if this was unintentional, your brain is more likely to seek that. Training our subconscious to seek pleasure and spend more time in a state of joy leads to more satisfaction.

When the universe puts nice things in your path, thank the universe. Make a habit of spending even a few minutes each day thanking the universe for its generosity. Write a gratitude journal, spend time with your family doing a daily gratitude exercise, or even reflect on your blessings over breakfast. Gratitude is part of happiness!

Thank Others

Every day we have events, situations, and people that have been the source of good cheer. It could be as simple as a coworker remembering our favorite cookie, your kids getting ready for school on time without a reminder, or your friend saving a seat for you on the subway. Make a note of all people who help you feel sunny and acknowledge those sources of joy.

While thanking the universe is an integral part of the internal process, the external process is equally important. Thank your friends, family, teachers, coworkers, or even total strangers. Anybody who is a source of joy deserves our expressions of gratitude. Your local government would love to hear that your life has dramatically improved with the new bus stop. It gives them the motivation to work on more demanding projects. Your friend would probably get a considerable happiness boost if you told them how valuable their lunch talks are to you. They are more likely to continue making time for those. The nurse looking after your mother deserves a thank you for remembering your mom's food preferences. They are more likely to engage intentionally in acts of kindness.

People deserve to feel seen and appreciated. Knowing that their actions, words, or acts of service brought happiness to someone can increase their happiness. They are more likely to keep putting out good cheer in the world when they know it makes a difference in the lives of others.

Additionally, expressing gratitude to individuals and establishments is another excellent way of practicing self-advocacy. As you frame what you are grateful for, you also frame what matters to you and why. It helps others understand what you care about and what part they can play in helping you with it.

Thank Yourself

One of the most critical acknowledgments we can make is to ourselves. Thank yourself for prioritizing happiness! It is not easy for everyone to take care of their own needs. It may not come naturally to all folks to advocate for their happiness. So if you're doing that, it deserves to be celebrated!

Prioritizing joy is no simple endeavor. It requires you to invest time, raise your awareness, create a plan, and be intentional about your actions. Whether you are doing big things like exercising during workdays for better health or small tasks like oiling the squeaky wheel under your chair, all of it deserves acknowledgment. Every action of prioritizing happiness is an act of self-advocacy. It is you doing something to address your needs.

Include yourself in your gratitude reflections. Pat yourself on the back when you make choices that are an investment in your happiness. Remind yourself why it matters that you chose joy and why you deserve it.

Acceptance

Welcoming joy in your life requires you to accept it. We can prioritize happiness only when we acknowledge that we deserve it, admit that our needs are valid, and ask others for help.

Accept Your Needs

What is important to you matters. Accepting that you have needs, preferences, and things that increase your joy is a meaningful way to live an authentic life.

It can be very uncomfortable for some people to acknowledge their needs, even to themselves. It may come from wanting to keep life simple and be satisfied, a fear of being seen as needy, being afraid of being disappointed in the gap between aspirations and reality, or something else entirely. In all cases, it is helpful to dig into that limiting belief and reframe your needs as an act of self-advocacy.

I've always loved a short commute. I didn't realize how critical that need for a quick commute was until the commute time dramatically increased. After five years in a job I loved, I moved locations, increasing my daily commute from twenty minutes to almost three hours. I lasted a year and then regretfully quit that job because my quality of life was taking a huge hit. Since then, filtering for location and commute time has been one of my most essential considerations when looking for a job. A long commute is a non-negotiable aspect for me and something I'm willing to trade other perks to obtain. My decision-making aligns with my priorities, making my life happier.

Accept Support

Happiness often requires us to receive help from others in case there are things that we can't control, but others can. It requires us to be vulnerable in sharing those needs and letting others be there for us.

In the workplace, it is great when asking for help or support is accepted. When workplaces encourage people to share their needs, speak up and ask for what they want, it creates a culture where making life better for everyone becomes normalized. If that culture isn't normalized in your workplace yet, you can help create that ethos by sharing what would be meaningful to bring more joy to your workday and asking for help. You might be surprised at people's willingness to help. Others can help you prioritize happiness if you speak up and make a good faith attempt to be reasonable.

Accepting support also means including others on your journey to prioritize joy and support them. It is always easier when a community of people shares your goal and helps you with it.

Accept Happiness

Happiness is not a zero-sum game. By being happy, you are not taking happiness from someone else. Accepting it today doesn't remove happiness tomorrow.

Keep reminding yourself of these things to eliminate the fear of accepting happiness. Someone else's sadness does not balance out our joy. Neither will our current pleasure cause us to be unhappy at a later stage. We may have cultural or social reasons for believing these things, but they are limiting beliefs with no basis in truth.

Happiness is a choice that we can all make. Plenty of people spend their whole life being happy, and I don't think they just got lucky the entire time. They chose options that gave them pleasure and intentionally prioritized joy. No tsunami happened because of their happiness, and no bouts of pain and sadness can be attributed to their moments of joy. Life can be short sometimes, so we must accept happiness and be joyful whenever possible.

Not everything is within our control, but plenty of things are. Being intentional and focusing on what you can control and where you can make shifts to attract more joy is investing in a healthier, happier you.

Action

After awareness, acknowledgment, and acceptance comes action. Create an intentional plan to prioritize happiness because it doesn't just happen by chance!

Refocus on Awareness

Spend enough time focusing on self-awareness and knowing what truly makes you happy.

- What increases your joy?
- How can you prioritize long-term happiness?
- What are you grateful for?

I did a fun exercise to create a chart of my happiness boosters. I am a data practitioner, so the fact that I made a chart should surprise nobody. Look at your past happy moments and try to break them down:

- The type of thing that made you happy
- The amount of effort required
- How long your happiness lasted

Although this assessment is subjective, the results can lead to surprising insights. The graph below shows some of my happiness boosters. I ranked them on the effort involved and the lasting effects on my well-being.

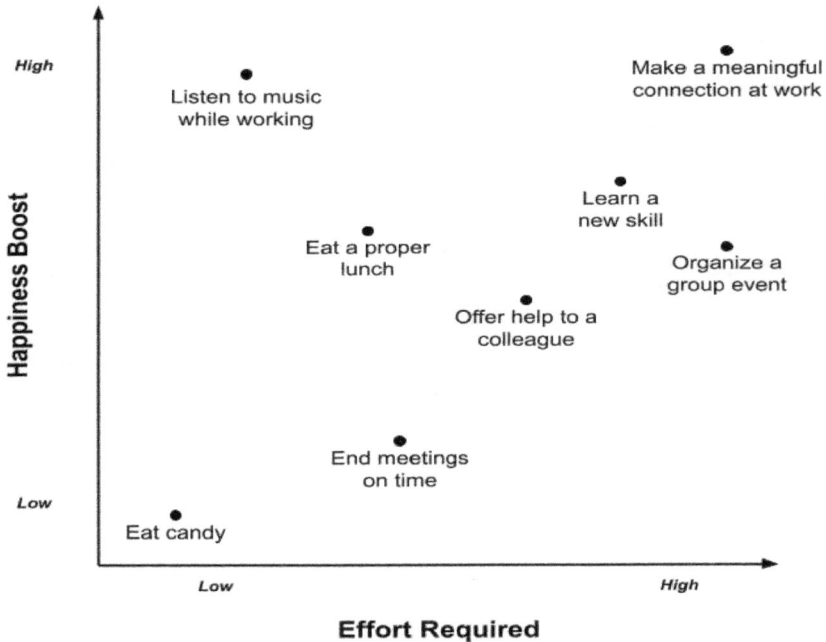

Effort Required

I'm essentially trying to maximize my happiness boost per amount of effort required. Your chart may look quite different. The idea is to be cognizant of what you value so it stays in your mind as something you need to prioritize.

What would your chart look like? Try it out and see what you come up with; you may be surprised by the results!

Create a Plan

Based on your assessment of happiness, come up with a plan. Outline strategies to address one action item that increases your joy for the next month. Or you could focus on a few action items and say you will try to prioritize at least one at any given point over the next three months.

Revisit Chapter 5 if you need help setting goals and keeping track of progress.

Take your goals and timelines seriously. After you write down your plans to improve your happiness, commit to maintaining your focus. Everything worth doing requires work!

When we face choices about how we will spend significant amounts of time, we must carefully weigh them against our happiness index. If there are big red flags that you know would cause frustration, look at other options or discuss ways in which you can mitigate them. Everything is negotiable.

Prioritizing happiness is a worthy goal to focus on in our professional lives. Some of our contentment is influenced by our work, and some by our personal life. Either way, we are whole people, which doesn't change when we go to work. Caring about our holistic happiness is an investment in our career as much as it is an act of self-advocacy.

Next Steps for Self-Advocacy

Connect with Me on Social Media

It would be wonderful to hear from you about your stories and progress on self-advocacy.

- What resonated from the book?
- What are your self-advocacy goals?
- What lessons from the book can you apply immediately?
- What recent wins are you ready to highlight?
- How can others help you on your self-advocacy journey?

Share anything you are comfortable with on social media. Tag me in your posts and I would love to amplify your journey and your wins!

#SelfAdvocacy

My LinkedIn: @ShailviW

Download Additional Resources on Self-Advocacy

All the worksheets and checklists found in this book are available to be downloaded from my website. I also include additional resources and update the content as needed. Scan the QR code (or type the link below) to access these resources:

www.shailvi.com/self-advocacy-resources.html

Acknowledgments

As a first-time author, writing a book was intimidating. Fortunately, I am lucky to have an incredible support system. I want to extend my gratitude to everyone who is part of it.

To my parents, Poonam and Col Satish Tyagi (Retd). I grew up admiring how you both showed up in your respective careers and the passion with which you advocated for yourself and others. You have made the world better. I love you both and owe you everything.

My sister Pallavi Tyagi always shows up for me with helpful feedback, optimism, and humor. My brother-in-law Anshuman Bhuchar's savviness and cheerleading are always reassuring and timely.

Extraordinary thanks to Amy Waninger. Your support in helping me publish this book has been priceless.

Alessandra Zielinski, you are an excellent coach. I feel lucky to have had you in my corner during critical times of my professional journey.

The content and tone of this book benefited greatly from early readers who were willing to offer their valuable feedback: Anam Abro, Kathleen Ragelis, Pallavi, Anshuman, and Govind. You were incredibly gracious with your time, and I am eternally grateful for your support.

My friend, Abhishek Gundugurthi, for gifting me my first book on women's leadership back in college. Kinjal, Rajit, Devika, Christine, Marco, Pushkar, Roopa, Anna, Ed, Shivam, Sibo, Prajakta, and Ramya: your friendship and support for all my projects have been invaluable. To all my friends, family, and well-wishers, thank you for being a part of my life and patiently listening to my musings on self-advocacy.

Grateful to several former colleagues and teammates for being sounding boards, supporters, and a source of intellectual stimulation. You helped me get this book across the finish line. Stephanie Pancoast and Danielle Guy - you've both been incredibly fantastic. I've had many great managers and people I learned from at work - thank you all.

Shoutout to Martin for introducing me to the weekly rating question, which I still use more than a decade later. I've also had many fantastic direct and skip-level reports who, especially in the last few years, have provided immediate feedback that made its way to the book. Thank you for the one-on-ones, slack conversations, and stimulating discussions over happy hours.

I also want to thank the coworkers, supervisors, and organizations that presented me with challenging situations over the years. They led me to grow my self-advocacy muscle. Without those lessons, I may not have authored this book.

I am in awe of the accomplished authors who were willing to speak with me and provide me with valuable advice. Lois Creamer, Karen Catlin, Stephanie Slocum, David Giltner, Dr. Oana Velcu-Laitinen, Deborah Anne Coviello, Dr. Deborah Thompson, Erin Thorp, Oscar Santolalla, Sara Wachter-Boettcher, Jyotika Singh, Julie Henry. And most of all, to Neil Thompson for connecting me to almost all the authors I mention.

I am grateful to all the wonderful people who have engaged with me on self-advocacy. You invited me to speak at conferences and corporate events. You came and heard my talk. You attended my workshops. You signed up for my mentoring sessions. You engaged with my content on LinkedIn and Twitter. You were early sign-ups for this book's waitlist. So many of you were vulnerable and willing to share your stories. So many of you offered feedback on my content. You all made me feel seen, and your acknowledgment meant the world. Thank you from the bottom of my heart! You are the inspiration for this book.

Finally, my most profound appreciation goes to my husband, Govind. Thank you for believing this book deserves to be out there from day one. Thank you for all your direct support that led to this book being written and published. And thank you for relentlessly reminding me never to settle for less than what I am worth!

About the Author

Shailvi Wakhlu is a Technology Leader and International Keynote Speaker. She is the former Head of Data & Analytics at Strava and Komodo Health. Her sixteen-year data and engineering career has included companies such as Salesforce, Fitbit, and a software startup she co-founded. Shailvi's self-advocacy expertise comes from being a practitioner at tech startups and large companies across three continents.

Wakhlu speaks on self-advocacy and data at twenty-five or more global conferences and Fortune 500 corporate events each year. She also teaches online courses on these subjects to a global audience.

Wakhlu offers individual and group coaching. She has helped hundreds of people grow their self-advocacy skills and reach important career milestones faster. She is also an investor and advisor to several high-growth startups.

Wakhlu grew up in India and studied Computer Engineering at Illinois Tech in Chicago. She loves to travel and has visited thirty-two countries. She lives in San Francisco with her husband, Govind, and their sixty plants.

www.shailvi.com
LinkedIn: @ShailviW